Don't Lose the Place!

A Comedy

Derek Benfield

A SAMUEL FRENCH ACTING EDITION

SAMUEL FRENCH

FOUNDED 1830

SAMUELFRENCH-LONDON.CO.UK
SAMUELFRENCH.COM

FOR AMATEUR PRODUCTION ENQUIRIES

UNITED KINGDOM AND WORLD
EXCLUDING NORTH AMERICA

plays@SamuelFrench-London.co.uk

020 7255 4302/01

Each title is subject to availability from Samuel French,

depending upon country of performance.

DON'T LOSE THE PLACE!

CHARACTERS
(in order of appearance)

Sylvia
Clive
Jemma
Walter
Eddie

The play takes place in Sylvia's flat overlooking the river in a fashionable suburb

ACT I   A Friday evening in the summer
ACT II   Five minutes later

Time — the present

Other plays by Derek Benfield published by Samuel French Ltd:

ACT I

Sylvia's artistically furnished flat is on the first floor overlooking the river in a fashionable suburb. Friday evening

Two wide steps UL lead to sliding glass doors which open on to a balcony, with a garden table and two chairs, from which a flight of steps leads down to the river. An archway UC leads to the front door and dining-room, and there are two bedroom doors side-by-side DL. Part of the kitchen is visible R and is reached through a door in a cut-away wall. In the kitchen there are kitchen units, a fridge, a small kitchen table and two chairs, and there is a way off to the rest of the kitchen UR. In the sitting-room there is a sofa LC with a coffee table on its R and a longer table above it. A small armchair DRC faces the television set, an apright chair against the wall DL, a drinks cupboard above the kitchen door and an oak chest above the bedroom doors

It is a pleasant summer evening and the sun is shining

When the CURTAIN rises, Sylvia is putting the finishing touches to the flat, obviously wanting it to be at its best. Romantic music is playing. Sylvia is a delightfully naïve young lady who, rather surprisingly for the time of day, is disturbingly dressed for bed. She re-arranges two wine glasses minutely, is better pleased, sighs happily, and goes out into Bedroom 1, walking on air

A young man appears outside, coming up the steps from the river. He is in rowing gear—white shorts and shirt, a rowing cap, and a sweater tied by the arms around his neck. This is Clive. He is a little breathless, and carries a box of chocolates

Clive peers in through the open glass doors, sees nobody there and comes in. He is obviously familiar with the surroundings. He sees an opened bottle of wine in an ice bucket on the table behind the sofa. He lifts it slightly, looks at the label and smiles, approvingly

Sylvia returns and is surprised to see him. She looks at her wrist-watch. The music stops

Sylvia What time do you call this?

Clive is somewhat taken aback by this reception, and he also looks at his watch

Clive A quarter past seven.
Sylvia You're not supposed to be here till seven-thirty.
Clive There was a strong tide running.
Sylvia You're a quarter of an hour early.
Clive Does it matter?
Sylvia I might not have been ready.
Clive (*smiling approvingly*) You *look* ready. You look *very* ready. And very nice ...
Sylvia (*playing hard to get*) But I might *not* have been. I might have been in the bath. Or gardening ...
Clive You haven't got a garden. You're on the first floor.
Sylvia I've got a window-box. I might have been out there — weeding. For all *you* knew.
Clive You can't get many weeds in a window-box. (*He holds out the box of chocolates*) These are for you.
Sylvia (*enthusiastically*) Oh, Clive! Chocolates! What a lovely surprise!
Clive I *always* bring them ...
Sylvia You're like that man in the ad on television — racing through all kinds of perils to reach your lady love with a box of chocolates! (*She opens the box and takes a chocolate*)
Clive Do you mind if I sit down? It's quite tiring rowing up the river.
Sylvia (*eating*) I thought you said there was a strong tide running.
Clive It's still a mile and a half from the boathouse.
Sylvia Well you'd *better* sit down, then. We don't want you to be too tired, do we?

Clive looks at her, and they smile sheepishly

Clive No. That would never do ... (*He sits down*)
Sylvia Would you like to have a drink first? (*She goes to pour the wine*)
Clive (*grinning*) We usually do.
Sylvia Oh, dear. You don't think we're getting into a rut, do you?
Clive If we are it's a rut I'd like to get into more often!

Sylvia Now, Clive — we mustn't be greedy.
Clive I wouldn't call once a fortnight overdoing it exactly.

Sylvia arrives with two glasses of wine and sits beside him

Thanks.

They raise their glasses

Sylvia Well ... here we go again!
Clive Yes — rather!

They drink, then put down their glasses, grab each other impulsively and go into a big kiss. Afterwards, they sit back, contentedly, his arm around her

You know ... there's something I'd really like to do one day when I come here ...
Sylvia (*giggling*) I thought that's what we *had* been doing ...!
Clive I'd like to arrive at the front door!
Sylvia Why?
Clive Well, I feel so furtive rowing up the river, tying up the boat and creeping up those bloody little steps!

Sylvia looks hurt

Sylvia It's supposed to be romantic ...
Clive (*grudgingly*) Yes. Yes, I know that. But what if we're still doing all this in the winter.
Sylvia You don't have to do "all this" at all, if you don't want to!
Clive Well, surely you don't expect me to come rowing a mile and a half up the river in the freezing cold? By the time I'd thawed out and got my working parts moving again it'd be time to go home.
Sylvia (*sulking a little*) If you don't want to go on, you only have to get back into your little boat and row away into the sunset. (*She goes to get a dish of nuts from the drinks cupboard*)
Clive Of course I want to go on! You know that. I want to go on more often. How about once a week? I wouldn't have thought once a week was asking too much.

Sylvia Nuts! (*She proffers the dish of nuts*)

Clive What? Oh. Thanks. (*He takes some nuts*)

Sylvia If we did it once a week it might become a habit.

Clive What's wrong with that?

Sylvia I might *think* I love you more than I do. I've got to be sure. I don't want to think I love you just because you've become a habit.

Clive If you marry me it soon *will* be a habit.

Sylvia That's the trouble. I don't know if I *want* to marry you.

Clive What?!

Sylvia Well, marriage is so ... permanent.

Clive I'd prefer to be permanent than once a fortnight!

Sylvia (*sitting beside him again*) Clive ... I've got to be sure. We might not ... like each other ... more than once a fortnight.

Clive At this rate we'll never know! (*He finishes his wine, abruptly*) Can I have some more wine?

Sylvia Already?

Fed up, Clive plods away to pour himself some more wine. Quite a pause

I hope you're not becoming an alcoholic.

Clive (*trying to be patient*) Sylvia ... I ... I merely want another small glass of weak white wine. That does not mean that I hide bottles in the greenhouse.

Sylvia I'm sorry you think my wine glasses are small. I didn't know you were used to drinking out of a bucket. Are you trying to tell me that before you make love to me you've got to be drunk?

Clive No, of course not! It's just that —

Sylvia And I'm sorry to hear you describe Sainsbury's Reisling as weak white wine.

Clive I meant no offence to Sainsbury's! It's a perfectly acceptable wine.

Sylvia I'm glad to hear it. (*A pause*) Clive ...

Clive (*abruptly*) Yes?

Sylvia If we *were* married ...

Clive puts down his glass and hastens back to her

Clive Well, that's something! At least you're saying "If".

Sylvia If we *were* married, we might not be able to afford a bottle of Sainsbury's weak white wine *every* night ...

Clive Well, maybe after we'd practised a little we'd be able to manage without artificial aids!

They laugh, happy again

Sylvia Oh, I do love you ...!
Clive Well, kiss me, then!

They kiss. The front doorbell rings. They both look alarmed

You're not expecting somebody, are you?
Sylvia No! Not today ...
Clive (*puzzled*) What do you mean "not today"?
Sylvia Er — not *now*! Don't worry. I'll get rid of them.
Clive But why did you say not today? Why not just no?

The doorbell goes again. She pulls him to his feet quickly

Sylvia You'd better wait in the kitchen while I see who it is!
Clive Why? There's nothing wrong with my being here, is there?
Sylvia Dressed like that? Quickly! (*She bundles him into the kitchen*) And Clive ...
Clive Yes?
Sylvia (*with a smile*) Don't lose the place!

She shuts the kitchen door and goes out into the hall

Clive sits, disconsolately. Lights out in the kitchen

(*Off*) Jemma!
Jemma (*off*) Oh, good! You recognized me.

Jemma walks in from the hall. She is an attractive, fashionably dressed career woman with a dry sense of humour. She is carrying a small suitcase and a plastic duty free bag. Sylvia follows her in, gazing at her in disbelief

Sylvia You're in France!
Jemma I don't *think* so ...

Sylvia You're coming back tomorrow!
Jemma No. I'm coming back today. In fact I think I've already arrived. This is number six, isn't it?

She disappears, quickly, into the hall and returns at once, smiling

Yes, it is, so I have.
Sylvia You said you were coming back tomorrow.
Jemma I know. But I caught a later plane today instead of an early plane tomorrow. Is it all right if I come in? I feel like a man selling brushes standing here.
Sylvia Er ... yes. I suppose so ...

Jemma moves into the room. Sylvia hovers anxiously

Jemma You must try not to be so over-whelming with your welcome. It might go to my head. (*She puts down her things and looks at Sylvia in surprise*) You weren't just going to bed were you?
Sylvia Well, I ... I was thinking about it ...
Jemma Bit early, isn't it?
Sylvia I've just had a bath.
Jemma Oh, good. You know what I'm like about personal hygiene. (*She is about to sit on the sofa*)
Sylvia (*sharply*) What are you doing?

Jemma freezes, her bottom poised a few inches above the sofa

Jemma I was going to sit down. I thought that's what sofas were for.
Sylvia You can't!
Jemma I *have* done it before. (*She sinks, gratefully, onto the sofa*)

Sylvia casts a nervous look towards the kitchen

I've had a wonderful trip! I've come back with masses of ideas. I felt like an industrial spy, making notes and drawing diagrams in all those posh fashion houses —
Sylvia Jemma!
Jemma Yes?
Sylvia Couldn't we talk about that tomorrow?

Jemma Oh — yes, of course. I'm sorry. I can see you're simply longing
to get to bed. I'll tell you all about it over breakfast. (*She gets up and
heads for the kitchen*)
Sylvia No!

Jemma stops and looks back at her, surprised

Jemma I beg your pardon?
Sylvia Where are you going?
Jemma Into the kitchen. I thought I'd make myself a cup of coffee.
Sylvia Not in there!
Jemma Don't tell me you've moved the kitchen? It was through there last
time I stayed.
Sylvia Yes ... yes, it is, but ...
Jemma That's what I thought. (*She starts again*)
Sylvia No! (*She leads Jemma back to the sofa*) I'll get it. You're far too
exhausted.
Jemma It's not very tiring making a cup of instant coffee.
Sylvia I insist! After all, it is my kitchen.

She sits Jemma down again, rather abruptly

There we are! You sit down and relax. It's such a *long* way from
France.
Jemma I didn't walk.
Sylvia You walked from the arrival gate to the luggage carousel, and
that's a *very* long way.
Jemma (*thoughtfully*) Yes, it *is*, isn't it ...?
Sylvia So you stay there — and I'll get the coffee!

*Sylvia goes to the kitchen door, opens it narrowly, squeezes through and
closes it behind her*

Jemma cannot understand Sylvia's behaviour

*Lights up in the kitchen. Clive is slumped in his seat. He looks up as Sylvia
comes in*

It's Jemma!

Clive Who the hell's Jemma?
Sylvia Ssh! She's my partner in the dress shop. I'll just put the kettle on.

Sylvia disappears into the hidden part of the kitchen

Clive gazes at her in amazement as she returns

Clive What are you putting the kettle on for?
Sylvia I'm making her a cup of coffee.
Clive (*appalled*) Why?
Sylvia (*putting some instant coffee into a mug*) Because she's very tired
  after walking all the way from the arrival gate to the luggage carousel.
Clive She's tired! I've rowed a mile and half up the bloody river!
Sylvia Keep your voice down! (*She gets some biscuits out of a tin and puts
  them on to a plate*)
Clive Why?
Sylvia Well, I don't want Jemma to know you're here, do I?
Clive What difference does it make?
Sylvia Ssh!
Clive (*a little quieter*) Can't you get rid of her?
Sylvia No. She's staying here.
Clive (*loudly*) Staying here?!

In the sitting-room, Jemma looks up, not sure if she has heard voices

Sylvia Ssh!
Clive (*quieter again*) Staying here?
Sylvia Yes. I lend her my spare room whenever she's in London.

Clive stares at her in horror

Clive So ... so what are we going to do?
Sylvia You'll just have to wait in here until she goes to bed.
Clive (*glancing at his watch*) It's only half-past seven! She won't go to
  bed for hours!
Sylvia Ssh!

*Jemma gets up, curiously, and goes across to the kitchen door. She puts
one ear against it*

Clive Can't you just *tell* her?

Sylvia Tell her what?

Clive About us! Tell her it's a bit inconvenient and pack her off to a hotel for the night!

Sylvia I couldn't do that. She'd be so embarrassed. Darling, it's only one evening.

Clive But I only *get* one evening! One evening once a bloody fortnight!

Sylvia Oh, good!

Clive What?

Sylvia The kettle's boiling.

Sylvia takes the mug of instant coffee granules into the back of the kitchen, returning after a moment with the coffee now made

Clive watches her, miserably, as she puts milk into the coffee

Don't worry, darling. I'll try and get her to go to her room. Then we can carry on from where we left off.

Clive Left off? We hadn't even started. (*He drifts away, doubtfully*) Anyway ...

Sylvia Anyway what?

Clive Well ... (*He looks far from enthusiastic*)

Sylvia Don't you want to?

Clive Of course I want to! But ... but it's supposed to be something between consenting adults in private, not with a lodger in the spare room.

Sylvia giggles, kisses him quickly and goes towards the door. Jemma races back to the sofa and hastily assumes a relaxed position as Sylvia comes in with the coffee and plate of biscuits

Clive sits down in despair. Lights out in the kitchen

Jemma Oh, thank you, Sylvia. That *is* kind. (*She takes the coffee and looks at Sylvia with a thoughtful smile*) Everything ... all right out in the kitchen?

Sylvia Oh —yes. Fine. (*Abruptly*) Would you like a biscuit? (*She thrusts the plate of biscuits at Jemma*)

Jemma A biscuit! How lovely! (*She takes one*) It's a funny thing, you know, but I could have sworn I heard voices.

Sylvia V-voices?
Jemma Yes. V-voices. In the k-kitchen.
Sylvia Ah — yes! That was me! I ... I was talking to myself. I often talk
to myself. In the kitchen.
Jemma Oh, I see ...

A pause

Sylvia (*abruptly*) Jemma — you must be so *tired*!

Jemma looks rather surprised

Jemma Perhaps I'll be more alert when I've had my coffee.
Sylvia (*warily*) Will you?
Jemma Well ... caffeine.
Sylvia It's Hag.
Jemma Sorry?
Sylvia Decaffeinated.
Jemma Then I shall have to concentrate on what's going on, won't I? Try
to keep my eyes open.
Sylvia Oh, you needn't do that! Not on account of me.
Jemma It would be awfully rude to fall asleep in the middle of coffee.
Even decaffeinated.
Sylvia Oh, I'll quite understand! You pop off to bed as soon as you like.
I've ... I've got things to see to. So I can see to them.
Jemma What things?
Sylvia Oh ... domestic things.
Jemma (*alarmed*) Hoovering?
Sylvia Oh, no! Quiet things. Very quiet. You won't even know that I'm
doing them. (*Then, anxiously*) You're not a light sleeper, are you?
Jemma Oh, no. Like a log.
Sylvia Oh, good!
Jemma But I wasn't thinking of going to bed at half-past seven.
Sylvia You don't have to worry about *me*! I'll be quite happy — getting
on with things in here. Would you like another biscuit?
Jemma Er — no, thanks. I had a meal on the plane.
Sylvia I'll put them away, then.

*Lights up in the kitchen as Sylvia goes to the kitchen door with the plate
of biscuits, opens it narrowly as before, squeezes through and closes it*

behind her. Jemma looks surprised, and concentrates on her decaffein-
ated coffee. Clive looks up as Sylvia comes in

Clive Has she gone to bed?
Sylvia Not yet! She's drinking her coffee. (*She goes to put the biscuits*
back in the tin)
Clive Well, you shouldn't have made it so hot! She'll be sitting there
sipping away for hours!
Sylvia Ssh!

In the sitting-room, Jemma looks up from her coffee, having heard voices
again. She puts down her coffee and trots across to listen at the door again

You'll just have to be patient, darling. It won't be for long. She's bound
to nod off soon, and then we can get on with it ...

Clive tries to be immune to her nearness

Clive I don't want to get on with it! Not now. I've gone off the idea.
Sylvia (*cuddling up to him*) Oh, Clive ... she says she sleeps like a log ...
Clive I'd still know she was there! It's no good. I'm going!

He starts to get up, but she pushes him down again

Sylvia You can't go out there!
Clive All right, then — you go and get rid of her! I'll give you two minutes
— and then I'm coming out! (*He glares at his watch*)
Sylvia No — you mustn't! (*She goes towards the door*)

In the sitting-room, Jemma races back to the sofa and hastily assumes a
relaxed position again as Sylvia returns

Jemma Lovely coffee.
Sylvia Oh. Good.

Trying to appear nonchalant, and yawning a little, Sylvia goes to the
windows and draws the curtains. The sitting-room darkens a little. Jemma
looks rather surprised

Jemma What on earth are you doing?

Sylvia The evenings are certainly drawing in, aren't they?

Jemma What are you talking about? It's the middle of summer. It won't be dark till ten.

Sylvia Really? We must be in for a storm, then. (*She looks out between the closed curtains*) Oh, yes! Masses of black clouds over there! It looks like the monsoon.

Jemma Sylvia — the sun's scorching down.

Sylvia Is it?

Jemma Are you feeling all right?

Sylvia I *was* ...

Jemma Perhaps you'd better sit down for a minute?

Sylvia No. I'm all right. Really.

Jemma (*as if to a child*) Then let's draw the curtains back again, shall we?

Sylvia Oh. Yes. Right. (*She draws the curtains back again*)

The sitting-room lightens. Jemma sips her coffee. Sylvia goes to her, briskly

Have you finished your coffee?

She starts to take away Jemma's coffee mug before she has finished. Jemma follows the mug, holding on to it, and finishes the coffee

Jemma I have *now* ...

Sylvia I'll clear the mug away.

Jemma Why don't *I* go this time?

Sylvia Sorry?

Jemma I want to know what's so fascinating about your kitchen. You don't seem able to keep out of it.

Sylvia No, no —I'll go!

Sylvia smiles, nervously, and goes into the kitchen, opening the door narrowly and squeezing through as before. Jemma watches her go, puzzled. Clive looks up from his watch as Sylvia comes racing in and goes to put down the mug

Clive Have you got rid of her?

Sylvia Give me a chance!

Clive Right! (*He gets up*)
Sylvia No! One more minute!

She scuttles out into the sitting-room again. Clive goes, determinedly, into the hidden part of the kitchen. Lights out in the kitchen

Jemma looks up in surprise as Sylvia comes racing back in

(*Abruptly*) Would you like to go for a walk?
Jemma A ... a walk? *Now?*
Sylvia Yes!
Jemma With you dressed like that?
Sylvia Ah ...
Jemma If you want some fresh air, why don't we go out and sit on the balcony? (*She starts to go*)
Sylvia No! You don't want to go out there!
Jemma But it's a lovely evening, and there's such a beautiful view of the river.
Sylvia You've seen it before! The river was there last time you stayed.
Jemma Oh, come on — we can watch the people rowing.
Sylvia No!
Jemma (*astonished*) What?
Sylvia You ... you'll embarrass them. I know people who row, and they ... they get embarrassed if you watch them.
Jemma Only if they're sinking.

Whereupon Clive walks out of the kitchen. He is now wearing a gentleman's raincoat over his rowing gear, his bare legs protruding from the bottom of it. Jemma stares at him in astonishment. Sylvia is frozen with fear. Clive stands there for a moment, feeling rather stupid. Then he starts to edge sideways like a crab towards the balcony. Jemma looks at Sylvia, inquiringly

Sylvia ...?

Sylvia finds her voice

Sylvia (*blurting out*) Will it be all right now?
Clive (*blankly*) Sorry?

Sylvia The ... the ball-cock.
Clive What?
Sylvia In the ... (*She indicates the kitchen*)
Clive (*realizing*) Ah!
Jemma (*to Sylvia*) I didn't know you'd got a ball-cock.
Sylvia Everybody's got a ball-cock!
Jemma Yes, but not usually in the kitchen.
Clive Yes! Yes, it's ... it's rising again now.
Jemma That *must* be a relief ...!
Clive So I ... I'll say good-night, then.
Sylvia (*disappointed*) Oh. Are you going?
Clive (*giving her a hard look*) Not much point in my staying here *now*,
    is there?
Jemma No. Not if it's rising again.
Clive Right. I'll be on my way (*He starts to go out on to the balcony*)
Jemma (*to Sylvia*) What about the bill?
Sylvia Sorry?
Jemma The bill for the ball-cock! You can't let him go without paying
    the bill for the ball-cock.
Clive Oh, never mind. I'll ... I'll send it.
Jemma Not cash on delivery?
Clive (*quietly*) I *didn't* deliver...!
Jemma What?
Clive Good-night, then, miss. (*To Jemma*) Good-night, ma'am.

*He gives a half-salute and scuttles out, disappearing down the steps to
the river*

Jemma turns to look at Sylvia with an inquiring smile

Sylvia The ... the plumber.
Jemma I'd never have guessed. Is he expecting a thunderstorm?
Sylvia Sorry?
Jemma He seems to be dressed for a downpour.
Sylvia It ... it was raining when he arrived.
Jemma (*giggling*) I say — did you notice his trousers?
Sylvia I wasn't looking at his trousers.
Jemma I'm not surprised. He didn't seem to have any on.
Sylvia He ... he probably got them wet in the rain. So he rolled them up

... under his coat. I expect he's caught a dreadful cold. The poor man was soaking.

Jemma Is that why you gave him a glass of wine?

Sylvia looks at her, frozen for a moment

Sylvia What?

Jemma Well — there are two glasses over here.

Sylvia I ... I felt so rude, drinking alone. So I offered him a glass. Only polite.

Jemma Very grand, white wine in an ice bucket, just for you and the plumber.

Sylvia He was very grateful.

Jemma I'm sure he was. It must have been such a surprise for him arriving to fix your ball-cock and finding you dressed like that offering him cold white wine. No wonder he managed to make it rise again.

Sylvia Would *you* like a glass of wine?

Jemma I thought you wanted me to go to bed.

Sylvia Oh, there's no hurry. (*Quietly, sadly*) Not *now* ...

Jemma Sylvia ...?

Sylvia Yes?

Jemma Does the plumber always leave through the window?

Sylvia Oh — no. It's just that he ... he came here by boat.

Jemma Aah! Like the river police?

Sylvia Yes!

Jemma Well, I suppose plumbers always *are* fond of water, aren't they?

Sylvia Yes. I suppose they are.

Jemma Funny ... I didn't know you could get jet lag flying from France, but I think I have ...! I'll go and unpack. (*She collects up her things*)

Sylvia Perhaps you'd like a bath?

Jemma Oh, thank you. That would be lovely. (*She crosses to the bedrooms, then stops and looks back at Sylvia*) I can't think why you didn't *say* you had a plumber in the kitchen with his trousers rolled up.

Sylvia Ah — yes — well ...

Jemma Look — I'm going to have my bath — and then you're going to tell me *exactly* what's going on here!

Jemma grins and goes out into Bedroom 2

Sylvia hastens to pour herself another glass of wine. The front door slams

Walter (*off*) Sylvia! You in?

Sylvia freezes in horror

Sylvia Oh, my God ...!

Walter walks in from the hall. He is a brisk, charming, successful businessman in his early fifties. He carries a bulging briefcase and a bunch of flowers, and is obviously thoroughly familiar with the surroundings. He sees Sylvia

Walter Hallo, darling!

Sylvia stares at him in alarm

Walter puts down his briefcase and looks, anxiously, at his wrist-watch

Sylvia Walter!

Walter waves a paw at her

Walter Not too late, am I? (*He heads for the television set*)
Sylvia Late?
Walter For the match. (*He switches the set on*)
Sylvia Walter ... (*She moves towards him with her wine*)

He chuckles, waving a finger at her, disapprovingly

Walter Ah-ha! You know I hate white wine. Oh — these are for you. (*He thrusts the flowers onto her, unceremoniously, and heads for the kitchen*)
Sylvia Where are you going?
Walter Grab myself a beer.

He goes into the kitchen. Sylvia remains, frozen, clutching the wine and the flowers. Walter returns with a can of beer. He notices her négligé, and grins

Bit early for bed, isn't it, darling?

He slaps her affectionately on the bottom and goes to tune in the television, thoroughly at home

Sylvia Walter!
Walter Hmm?
Sylvia How did you get in?
Walter (*busy with the set*) Same way I always do. Put the key in the lock, turn it to the left and the door opens as if by magic.
Sylvia But where did you get the key?
Walter Usual place. Under the geraniums. That's where you always leave the spare key.
Sylvia I didn't mean to leave it there tonight ...
Walter Anything in the freezer? I didn't have time to eat, and I'm starving.

He settles himself down, facing the television, and turns up the volume a little. Football commentary is heard faintly

Walter Ah! Good! Just in time. (*He opens the can of beer with a noise like a pistol shot*) Y'know I've spent all day avoiding newspapers and conversations so I could enjoy the recording of the match tonight. (*He realizes that she is still hovering*) Anything the matter?
Sylvia Oh, no — nothing at all! (*She stands there seething*)

Walter thinks he knows what is troubling her

Walter Ah. Sorry. (*He gets up and goes to her*) Hallo, darling ... (*He kisses her, perfunctorily*) Aren't you going to put those in water?

Sylvia thumps the bunch of flowers down, abruptly, on the end of the sofa. Walter returns with his beer to sit facing the television again

Sylvia (*furious*) Walter!
Walter Hmm?
Sylvia What are you *doing* here?
Walter (*intent on the screen*) Look, darling — couldn't we talk *after* the match? You know I like to concentrate. (*He concentrates*)

Seething, Sylvia goes and turns off the television, abruptly. Walter gazes at her in horror

What are you doing? It's the third round of the UEFA Cup!
Sylvia I don't care if it's the final! They lost anyway.

He gazes at her, a broken man

Walter How could you do a thing like that to a man? After the time I've had at the office avoiding the result. I've been going about all day saying, "Don't tell me! I'm watching it tonight!"
Sylvia (*moving back to the wine*) Well, now you know the result you can go home, can't you?

Walter follows her, fed up

Walter You've ruined my evening. You know that, don't you?
Sylvia Walter, will you please *go*!
Walter I don't know what's got into you tonight. You're usually pleased to see me.
Sylvia Only when I'm expecting you! And I wasn't expecting you tonight.

Walter notices the bottle of wine in the ice-bucket

Walter White wine in an ice-bucket! Bit grand, isn't it? Sainsbury's *would* be pleased. Have you got company?
Sylvia No! No — of course not!
Walter What was the score?
Sylvia Three-nil.
Walter Oh, my God ...!

Sylvia glances anxiously towards the bedrooms

Sylvia Walter — *please* go ...
Walter I've only just arrived.
Sylvia But you're not due until Wednesday. I wasn't expecting you tonight.
Walter You look as if you were expecting *some*one! (*He chuckles and heads for the kitchen*)

Sylvia Where are you going?
Walter I'm starving! Surely you won't deny a bit of bread and cheese to a starving man?

Walter goes into the kitchen to ferret for food. Sylvia puts her glass down and is about to follow him

Clive appears, coming up the steps from the river, still in the raincoat

Sylvia reacts in alarm and hastily closes the kitchen door and goes to him, urgently

Sylvia Clive! I thought you'd gone!

Clive glances about cautiously

Clive Where's Jemma?
Sylvia Having a bath.
Clive That's all right, then. (*He takes off the raincoat*)
Sylvia What are you doing? You can't come back in here!
Clive But my boat's disappeared!
Sylvia What?!
Clive It must have slipped its moorings in the strong tide and drifted off! (*He turns away to put the raincoat down on a chair*) I'll have to stay here.

Sylvia remembers Walter's flowers. She panics, hastily picks them up and hides them behind her back

Sylvia No! You can't!
Clive What am I supposed to do, then? Swim a mile and a half up the bloody river?
Sylvia Ssh! (*She glances, nervously, towards the kitchen*)
Clive She can't hear us in the bath.
Sylvia You've never lost a boat before. It's bound to be out there somewhere!
Clive I tell you it's gone!
Sylvia It can't do any harm to have another look!
Clive (*reluctantly*) Oh, all right ...

He goes out on to the balcony and disappears down the steps. Sylvia quickly opens the drinks cupboard, flings the flowers inside, closes it again and races out on to the balcony. She disappears down the steps to the river

Walter comes back from the kitchen, munching at a hunk of bread and cheese. He is surprised to find Sylvia has gone, and moves towards the balcony, looking about for her

Walter Sylvia!

He notices the raincoat on the chair, picks it up and looks at it, smiles delightedly, and then puts it down again. He collects his beer, turns the television on and sits down to watch the match, gloomily, the result of which is now no surprise to him. We hear the commentary and cheering crowd faintly as he stares, mournfully, at the picture

Jemma comes in from Bedroom 2. She is now wearing attractive silk pyjamas

Jemma (*entering*) Well, I've had my bath and now I'm all ready for you!

She stops, seeing a man crouching in front of the television. Walter looks at her. They stare at each other for a moment, neither knowing who the other is

I suppose you must be the television repair man?
Walter Sorry?
Jemma Have you come to adjust her horizontal hold?
Walter Certainly not! Isn't eight o'clock a bit early to start taking your clothes off?
Jemma I've just got back from France.
Walter I didn't know everyone in France took their clothes off at eight o'clock.
Jemma I was looking for Sylvia.
Walter So was I. She seems to have disappeared. (*He chuckles*) I've heard of this sort of thing, you know.
Jemma What sort of thing?

Walter People in the suburbs, all ripping their clothes off before sunset. *(He laughs and concentrates on the television)*

Jemma Are you watching the UEFA Cup?

Walter Yes ... *(He concentrates, gloomily)*

Jemma They lost.

Walter I *know!*

Jemma Not much point in watching it, then, is there? *(She switches the set off)* Three-nil!

Walter glares at her. She smiles serenely

We haven't met before, have we?

Walter No. I think I'd have remembered you wearing pyjamas.

Jemma Does Sylvia know you're here? *(She goes to pour herself a glass of wine)*

Walter *(munching his bread and cheese)* Certainly. I'm not in the habit of breaking into strange houses to watch the television.

Jemma Was she ... expecting you?

Walter No.

Jemma I thought not ...!

Walter It was a surprise.

Jemma Yes, I bet it was ...!

Walter I happened to be passing, so I popped in.

Jemma You popped in and she popped out. I wonder where she's gone.

Walter I dunno. She was here when I went into the kitchen.

Jemma Ah! Perhaps the plumber came back for his money.

Walter *(puzzled)* Plumber?

Jemma He's been fixing her ball-cock.

Walter At this time of night? And you both dressed for bed?

Jemma *(thoughtfully)* Yes. *I* thought it was a bit odd, too ...

Walter So why are you wearing pyjamas?

Jemma *(coldly)* I've been having a bath.

Walter Haven't you got a bath in your own flat?

Jemma Of course I've got a bath!

Walter But you prefer to use other people's?

Jemma I'm a friend of Sylvia's!

Walter So am I, but I don't have a bath every time I visit her.

Jemma I've just got back from France.

Walter Oh. Well, that explains it. I hope you're not going home dressed like that?

Jemma I'm not going home. I'm staying here. And if my pyjamas bother you I'll take them off.

Walter looks at her beadily

Walter Are you trying to seduce me?
Jemma No fear!
Walter Don't sound so appalled. People *have* tried to seduce me in my time.
Jemma I'm very surprised to hear it.

Walter gets up and goes towards the kitchen

Where are you going?
Walter Well, if you're going to start ripping your clothes off before sunset I shall need another beer.

He grins and goes into the kitchen, closing the door behind him

Sylvia comes up the steps from the river, looking about anxiously

Jemma gives her a bleak stare

Jemma It's all right. He's gone into the kitchen.
Sylvia W-what?
Jemma He's helping himself to another beer.
Sylvia Oh. You ... you saw him, then?
Jemma I couldn't avoid him. I came in from my bath and there he was. You didn't tell me you were giving a party.
Sylvia I'm not! (*She sees the raincoat*) Oh, my God ...!

Sylvia hastens across to pick up the raincoat. She dithers for a moment, uncertainly, and then rolls it up into a ball and stuffs it under the front of the sofa. Jemma watches her in astonishment

Jemma What on earth are you doing?
Sylvia Tidying up. We've got guests.
Jemma So I noticed! Who is he?
Sylvia Er ... who?

Jemma The one in the kitchen!

Sylvia Oh, that's Walter. (*She smiles, ingenuously*)

Jemma Is he another plumber? You must be holding a convention.

Sylvia No, no — he's a solicitor. And solicitors do ask questions, so you'll have to keep him in the kitchen!

Jemma Will I?

Sylvia Yes!

Jemma Why?

Sylvia So I can let the other one out of the front door.

Jemma What other one?

Sylvia The one out there! (*She indicates the balcony*)

Jemma You mean the plumber? I thought he'd gone.

Sylvia So did I ...! And he isn't a plumber.

Jemma Then what was he doing fiddling about with your ball-cock?

Sylvia He teaches physical education at Roxborough College and his name's Clive.

Jemma And does he *always* travel by boat?

Sylvia Not any more! He's lost it.

Jemma Lost his boat?

Sylvia Yes. So, Jemma, I've got no choice — I'll have to let him out of the front door!

Jemma And you don't want Walter to see him going out of the front door?

Sylvia (*vehemently*) No, of course not!

Jemma considers this

Jemma Doesn't Walter like people going out of front doors?

Sylvia Walter doesn't know anything about Clive!

Jemma Neither do I. Apart from the fact that he's lost his boat and he isn't a plumber.

Sylvia fetches the bottle of wine and her own glass and brings them to Jemma

Sylvia Jemma — you're my oldest friend!

Jemma How very depressing. Don't you know anyone older than me?

Sylvia I mean you've been my friend the longest! We're partners.

Jemma So ...?

Sylvia So you've got to help me. (*She pours more wine into Jemma's glass*)

Jemma Don't worry. I'm sure we can finish the bottle between us.
Sylvia Help me to sort it all out!
Jemma Sort all what out?

Sylvia hastily pours some wine into her own glass

Sylvia I'll explain everything later —
Jemma Oh, good. Because I am a bit puzzled.
Sylvia But now I want you to go and keep Walter in the kitchen while I
    get Clive out of the front door.
Jemma Ah! You mean Clive doesn't *know* about Walter?
Sylvia Of course he doesn't!
Jemma Ah. I didn't know that.
Sylvia I'll tell you all about it in a minute. Just keep him in the kitchen!

*Sylvia finishes her drink quickly, puts down her glass, replaces the
bottle in the ice bucket as she races out on to the balcony and disappears
down the steps to the river*

Jemma watches in surprise

*Walter comes in from the kitchen with a fresh can of beer and catches a
brief glimpse of Sylvia as she goes*

Walter Was that Sylvia?
Jemma Sylvia? Where?
Walter Going down the steps to the river!
Jemma (*deliberately vague*) I didn't see anyone.
Walter Surely she's not paying the plumber in her nightdress? I'd better
    see if she's all right! (*He starts towards the balcony*)

*Jemma hastily puts down her wine glass, races across and intercepts him,
her arms outstretched*

Jemma No! You can't go out there!

Walter stares at her in surprise

Walter What?

Jemma The plumber's gone! Ages ago! Before you arrived. He's been. And gone.

Walter So what's Sylvia doing out there?

Jemma Looking at the sunset.

Walter In her nightclothes? (*He goes past her on to the balcony*)

Jemma Walter!!

Walter stops again and turns to look at her once more

Walter How do you know my name?

Jemma You ... you told me.

Walter No, I didn't. I don't go around getting on to first name terms with strange people in pyjamas.

Jemma Let's go into the kitchen! (*She grabs his arm and pulls him, abruptly, towards the kitchen*)

Walter What are you doing?

Jemma It's through here.

Walter I know where it is. I've just been there.

Jemma Well, let's go again. It's a very nice kitchen.

Walter It may be, but you can't keep going in and out of kitchens however nice they are.

Jemma We'll get you a can of beer.

Walter I've just got one! (*He holds it up*)

Jemma looks at the beer can as if it were the most pathetic thing she had ever seen

Jemma Oh, but you've got such a little one! Far too small for a big man like you.

Walter (*bewildered by her behaviour*) Are you all right?

Jemma I just want you to feel really at home.

Walter Even at home I only drink one can of lager at a time.

Jemma (*wheedling*) Oh, come on, Walter ...

Walter I beg your pardon?

Jemma Let's go into the kitchen. There's something I want to show you.

Walter Good God, you *are* trying to seduce me!

Jemma In the kitchen?

Walter I've heard what goes on in the suburbs.

Jemma I only want to show you the freezer!

Jemma pushes Walter out into the kitchen, glances anxiously towards the balcony, and then follows him out, closing the door behind her

Sylvia's head appears as she comes up on to the balcony. She looks inside to make sure that the coast is clear, then calls down to Clive, impatiently

Sylvia Come on, Clive! Hurry up!
Clive (*off*) All right! All right! I'm coming!

Sylvia looks anxiously towards the kitchen. A cry of agony from below as Clive slips on the steps. Sylvia looks down at him, alarmed

Sylvia Are you all right?
Clive (*off*) No, I'm *not* all right ...
Sylvia What have you done?
Clive (*off*) I think I've broken my bloody leg!

Sylvia reacts and hastily disappears down the steps again

Lights up in the kitchen. Walter is starting to seethe

Walter All right, I've looked at the freezer — *now* can I go back in there?
Jemma No! Not yet! (*Dramatically, her arms flung out*) Stay here with me!
Walter Have you gone mad? Who *are* you, anyway?
Jemma I'm Jemma! Sylvia's partner in the dress shop.
Walter Oh. How do you do.

He shakes hands politely, then starts to go

Jemma Where are you going?
Walter I'm not staying here staring at a freezer with a demented woman in silk pyjamas.

Jemma gets to the door first and removes the key

Jemma (*acting up*) Oh, Walter — don't leave me!

Walter cannot believe what is happening

Walter Now, look here — if you want to rape me, rape me in the bedroom.

They freeze

Outside, Clive's head appears. He is being pushed up the steps from below by Sylvia. He is groaning in agony

Clive Oooooo ...! Oooooo ...!

They arrive on the balcony, she supporting him. He hops into the sitting-room. Sylvia casts a nervous glance towards the kitchen

Sylvia Does it hurt?
Clive Of course it bloody well hurts! Help me to the sofa.
Sylvia You're not sitting on the sofa!
Clive Why not?
Sylvia Because you can't stay here!
Clive *(trying to be patient)* Sylvia ... my boat's disappeared and I've sprained my ankle ... what the hell do you mean I can't stay here?
Sylvia What about Jemma?
Clive She'll be in the spare room. I'll be on the sofa.
Sylvia No, you won't!

They freeze

In the kitchen ...

Walter Ah! There she is!
Jemma I didn't hear anything.
Walter Voices!
Jemma No!
Walter In the sitting-room!

He tries to get past her, but she won't let him

Jemma No! You can't go in there!
Walter There's someone in the sitting-room!

Jemma (*whispering, urgently*) Ssh! You must keep your voice down!
Walter Why the hell should I keep my voice down?

They freeze

In the sitting-room ...

Clive There's someone in the kitchen!
Sylvia It'll be the radio! I always leave the radio on in the kitchen. You must go!
Clive How *can* I go when my boat's gone?
Sylvia Through the front door!
Clive You expect me to go out into the street dressed like this and hop all the way home?
Sylvia Get a taxi!
Clive But my money's in my trousers and my trousers are in the boathouse!
Sylvia I'll lend you some money! (*She gets her handbag*)

Clive is about to sit on the sofa when she sees him and calls out to try and stop him

Clive ...!

But he has lost his balance

Clive Aaaaa ...!

He sits on the sofa, his bad leg sticking up in the air. She glares at him. They freeze

In the kitchen ...

Walter There's someone in the sitting-room!
Jemma It'll be the radio! Sylvia always leaves the radio on in the sitting-room.
Walter There were voices! Will you please get out of my way?

He pushes Jemma aside and tries to open the kitchen door, but it is locked. He looks at her and holds out his hand

Key, please ...

Jemma puts the key down her cleavage, and smiles at him

Jemma Come and get it.

They freeze

In the sitting-room ...

Clive There's someone trying to get out of the kitchen!
Sylvia It's only Jemma.
Clive Why has she locked herself in the kitchen?
Sylvia She's just got back from France. (*She goes to him with a ten-pound note*) Here you are — get a taxi!

She puts the money down on the coffee table and starts to pull him to his feet

Walter (*as before*) All right, Jemma — you asked for it!
Sylvia (*hearing the voice*) Oh, my God! Come on — quickly! (*She starts to lead Clive away*)
Clive *Now* where are we going?
Sylvia Back into the spare room!

She drags the bewildered Clive out into Bedroom 2, casting an anxious look back as they go

In the kitchen ...

Walter is advancing on Jemma. She retreats a little, uncertainly

Jemma Walter ...! You ... you wouldn't ...!
Walter You told me to.
Jemma But you wouldn't!
Walter Yes, I would.
Jemma W-would you?
Walter I might.

Jemma You're bluffing.

Walter Well, *I'm* prepared to risk it if *you* are. (*He starts to advance again*)

Jemma No! No! I'll get it!

Jemma looks for it down her cleavage, but she cannot find it

It's gone!

Walter What?!

Jemma (*searching, frantically, in her bosom*) I can't find it!

Walter Oh, no ...!

Jemma I had it a moment ago! I think I've lost it!

She pulls the front of her pyjama jacket away from her bosom and peers down her front, desperately

Walter Here — let *me* look!

Jemma No!

She puts her arms across her bosom, defensively. Then she gets a metal tray from beside the fridge and stands on it. She shimmies and shakes her body for a while until the key falls out with a clatter on to the tray. She picks it up, triumphantly, and goes to unlock the door. She opens the door and peers into the sitting-room. She is relieved to see that the coast is clear. They go into the sitting-room

Lights out in the kitchen. Jemma and Walter come into the sitting-room from the kitchen

Jemma You see? I told you. There's nobody here.

Walter wanders, looking about, very bewildered

Walter I could have sworn I heard Sylvia talking to somebody. Perhaps the plumber's still about?

Jemma No! I told you — he's gone!

Walter He must have gone in a hell of a hurry. He seems to have left his money behind. (*He picks up the ten-pound note and holds it aloft*) I'll see if he's still there ... (*He starts to go towards the balcony with the money*)

Jemma No! (*She races across and intercepts him, her arms outstretched*)

Walter What?

Jemma That's not the plumber's money!

Walter How do *you* know?

Jemma Sylvia's far too careful with money to leave ten pounds lying about for the plumber.

Walter Well, *some*body left ten pounds lying about. (*He chuckles, suspiciously*) Ah! So *that's* what's been going on here!

Jemma Sorry?

Walter Well, put yourself in my position! I arrive here unexpectedly and find Sylvia with her clothes off at a quarter to eight, hear a strange man in the sitting-room who mysteriously disappears, and then find ten pounds left on the sofa table! I'd better find out what's happening. (*He goes out on to the balcony*)

Jemma I don't see that it's any of your business!

Walter stops and looks back at her with a big grin

Walter Oh, yes, it is. I want to *marry* Sylvia.

Jemma reacts

Walter disappears down the steps to the river

Walter (*calling as he goes*) Sylvia! Sylvia ...!

Jemma Oh, no ...!

She moves away, appalled

Sylvia comes in from Bedroom 2 and slams the door. Jemma jumps a mile

Aah! Oh, it's *you*! I thought you were still out there!

Sylvia (*going to her*) What have you done with Walter?

Jemma Nothing, but it was touch and go. He's outside. Looking for you. Has the other one gone home?

Sylvia No. He's in the spare room.

Jemma He's not sleeping with me!

Sylvia (*laughing*) Of course he's not sleeping with you!

Jemma There's no need to say it like that.

Sylvia Like what?

Jemma As if *nobody* would want to sleep with me.

Sylvia Don't be silly. You've been sleeping with people for years.

Jemma Not people! One person. And I'm married to him.

Sylvia Doesn't it get rather boring?

Jemma What?

Sylvia Sleeping with the same person for years.

Jemma Oh, no. We've got a television in the bedroom.

Sylvia (*anxiously*) Walter didn't *see* Clive, did he?

Jemma No. He just saw ten pounds and thought you were selling your body.

Sylvia I was giving it to Clive.

Jemma What?!

Sylvia The money!

Jemma Why?

Sylvia Because he's sprained his ankle. So I gave him ten pounds for his taxi home.

Jemma So why is he still in the spare room?

Sylvia Because I had to wait till Walter was out of the way! Ring for a taxi, would you? I'll go and get Clive before Walter comes back. (*She starts to go*)

Jemma No!

Sylvia puts on the brakes

Sylvia What?

Jemma goes quickly out on to the balcony and looks down at the river

What are you doing? He'll be back in a minute!

Jemma No, he won't. He's staring at the river.

Sylvia (*alarmed*) He's not going to jump, is he?

Jemma (*returning*) I don't think suicide is quite Walter's style, somehow. Now! (*She grabs Sylvia's arm and leads her, purposefully, to the sofa*)

Sylvia What are we going to do?

Jemma plonks Sylvia down on the sofa, rather abruptly

Jemma You're going to tell me why you're hiding a strange young man in shorts in your spare bedroom while another man who says he wants to marry you is out there staring at the river!

Sylvia Couldn't I tell you later? (*She tries to escape*)

Jemma No! (*She pulls her back on to the sofa*) You tell me *now*!

Sylvia (*with difficulty*) Well ... well, it was all *your* fault!

Jemma Yes. I thought it would be.

Sylvia It was *you* who told me to start picking over the possibles!

Jemma When did I do that?

Sylvia After I left Robin.

Jemma You didn't leave Robin. *He* left *you*.

Sylvia (*ignoring this*) Anyway, that's when you said it.

Jemma I only said there were hundreds of other fish in the sea. I just didn't want you fretting over the one that got away.

Sylvia Well, I took your advice. And that's what I've been doing — casting my nets!

Jemma embraces her, delightedly

Jemma Oh, I *am* glad! You're going to be married!

Sylvia (*uncertainly*) Well ...

Jemma Thinking about it?

Sylvia Yes.

Jemma And Walter's the lucky man?

Sylvia N ... no ...

Jemma No?

Sylvia He's *one* of them.

Jemma One of them ?!

Sylvia Yes.

Jemma Sylvia ... in this country people usually get married in pairs. You know — one of each sex. Well, usually one of each sex. One man and one woman. One pink and one blue. It's a sort of ... tradition.

Sylvia (*laughing*) I know that!

Jemma But you said Walter was *one* of them.

Sylvia One of the ... contenders.

Jemma You make it sound like a boxing tournament. (*She indicates Bedroom 2*) And is Hopalong Cassidy another contender?

Sylvia Yes ...

Jemma I thought he might be.

Sylvia gets up and runs out on to the balcony to peer down at Walter

Jemma Has he jumped?

Sylvia No. Still staring. *(Returning, thoughtfully)* You see, the trouble is that I can't make up my mind who I want to marry if I can't marry Robin. I just haven't met the perfect man.

Jemma Well, there aren't many of those about ...

Sylvia There are things I love about Walter and things I love about Clive. If only I could take bits of one and bits of the other and put them all together ...

Jemma Like Frankenstein's monster?

Sylvia You know what I mean!

Jemma Well, you're going to *have* to make up your mind, aren't you?

Sylvia I can't ! So I thought I'd ... try them out.

Jemma Try them out? You're talking about marriage, not a mail order catalogue!

Sylvia It's the same sort of thing. When people come into our shop they don't buy the first dress they see, do they? They ... try on a few. For size.

Jemma *(going to her, astounded)* And that's what you're doing? Trying them for size!

Sylvia Well ... in a way.

Jemma *Now* I suppose you're going to tell me that you've made out a roster! One this week, one next week ...

Sylvia Yes.

Jemma You *have*?!

Sylvia Yes. And usually it works out all right. But tonight they got ... mixed up a bit. I wasn't expecting Walter tonight.

Jemma And do they know you're just trying them for size?

Sylvia Of course not! I couldn't tell them that, could I? Walter doesn't know about Clive, and Clive doesn't know about Walter.

Jemma No wonder you didn't want them to meet!

Sylvia So, Jemma — whatever happens, they mustn't find out about each other!

Outside, Walter arrives on the balcony from the river and ambles into the sitting-room

Walter Lovely view out there ... *(He sees Sylvia)* Ah — I've been looking for you!

Jemma Well, you'd hardly find her down by the river in her dressing-gown, would you?

Sylvia Have you met Jemma?

Walter Yes, I have! She tried to seduce me in front of the freezer. Who were you talking to in here?

Sylvia To — to Jemma, of course!

Walter No, no! When Jemma and I were in the kitchen! It sounded like a *man's* voice.

Jemma (*mocking disappointment*) You mean you were listening to voices in here when I was trying to seduce you out there? I'm quite hurt. You might at least have been paying attention ...

Walter (*to Sylvia*) Well? Who was it?

Sylvia It ... it was the plumber.

Jemma (*whispering, urgently*) No, it wasn't!

Sylvia What?

Walter *She* told me the plumber went ages ago.

Sylvia Did you?

Jemma Yes, I did ...!

Sylvia Well, he came back.

Jemma What?

Sylvia To collect his money!

Walter The plumber doesn't seem to be able to keep his mind on the job. Came back to collect his money and then went off without it! (*He waves the ten-pound note in the air*)

Sylvia Ah — no— that's not the plumber's money!

Jemma That's what I told him.

Walter Then who does it belong to?

Jemma The window-cleaner!

Sylvia and Walter look at her in surprise

Sylvia }
Walter } (*together*) Window-cleaner?!

Jemma Yes!

Walter At this time of night?

Jemma He — he was late! He should have been here ages ago. She was expecting him this afternoon. Weren't you?

Sylvia (*blankly*) Was I?

Jemma Of course you were!

Sylvia Of course I was! (*to Walter*) That's why I left ten pounds in here.
Walter Oh, I see. (*He puts the money down on the coffee table*)
Jemma (*to Sylvia*) Walter thought it was your immoral earnings.
Sylvia Ten pounds! Is that all you think I'm worth?
Walter You'll never guess what *else* I found in here.

Jemma and Sylvia exchange an apprehensive look, then turn back to Walter

Jemma ⎫
              ⎬ (*together*) What?
Sylvia ⎭
Walter My raincoat!

The girls exchange another look

Jemma ⎫
              ⎬ (*together*) Raincoat?
Sylvia ⎭
Walter I've been looking for it everywhere. (*Crossing to the chair where he left it*) I couldn't think where I'd left it — and it was here in your flat all the — (*He stops, finding that it is no longer there*) That's funny. Seems to have disappeared ...
Sylvia You — you must have imagined it!
Walter (*going to them*) How could I imagine a raincoat? It was here, I tell you!
Sylvia Well, *I* didn't see it! Did you, Jemma?
Jemma I'm not sure ... What sort of raincoat was it? Gabardine?
Walter Yes.
Jemma Sort of beige?
Walter Yes.
Jemma With a belt?
Walter Yes!
Jemma No, I didn't see it.
Walter (*looking about*) Must be here somewhere ... (*He sees something*) Good heavens ...!

Walter goes down on to his knees and peers under the sofa. He pulls the raincoat out and looks up at them in astonishment

Funny place to put a raincoat. All screwed up under the sofa!

Sylvia (*heavily surprised*) Oh — is that *your* raincoat?

Walter Of course it is!

Sylvia We wondered who it belonged to. Didn't we, Jemma?

Jemma Well, *you* did. I wasn't bothered ...

Sylvia And it was yours all the time! Well, well ...

Walter Surely you *knew*?

Jemma Of course she didn't know. All raincoats look alike. It might have been anybody's.

Walter (*to Sylvia*) Do you have lots of men who leave their raincoats behind? Are there three or four of these stuffed under the sofa? (*He looks under the sofa*)

Sylvia No! Of course not! I ... I just didn't recognize it.

Walter gets up and looks at his raincoat, sadly

Well, you wouldn't recognize it *now*! It's all creased ...

Jemma Oh, don't fuss, Walter! It'll soon hang out. (*She grabs the raincoat from him and flaps it about a bit*)

Clive comes hopping out of Bedroom 2

Clive Are you going to keep me waiting in the bedroom all night?

He stops, seeing Walter. And Walter sees him. Sylvia and Jemma are frozen, Jemma holding the raincoat like a matador

Walter (*finally*) I suppose you must be the window-cleaner?

Clive Sorry?

Walter I've never seen a window-cleaner in shorts before.

Clive I'm not a window-cleaner!

Walter (*holding up the ten-pound note*) This isn't *your* money, then?

Clive Well ... she did offer it to me.

Walter What?!

Jemma and Sylvia exchange an anguished look. Walter goes to Clive

Sylvia offered you money?

Clive Yes.

Walter Even though you aren't a window-cleaner?

Clive Yes.

Walter What are you, then? Some sort of gigolo?

Sylvia (*suddenly*) For a taxi!

Walter Why should you give him money for a taxi?

Jemma Well, he could hardly hop all the way home, could he?

Walter I can't think what he was doing hopping about in here in shorts in the first place!

Clive What's it got to do with you where I hop about in shorts?

Walter Look, I happen to be — !

Sylvia Walter !!

Walter and Clive look at her in surprise. Jemma hastily comes to her aid

Jemma Yes. He happens to be Walter.

Clive Who the hell's Walter?

Walter I am! Sylvia—if this man in shorts *isn't* the window-cleaner what he hell is he doing here?

Clive glares at Walter, and is about to speak, but Sylvia gets in first

Sylvia That's just what *I* was thinking!

They all look at her for a moment. Then she turns to Jemma in assumed outrage

    Jemma!

Jemma cowers, uncertain of what is to come

Jemma Y-yes?

Sylvia You never told me he was still here!

Naturally, Jemma has no idea what Sylvia is talking about. Nor has Clive! Jemma dithers, in limbo

Jemma I beg your pardon?

Sylvia Clive! He's still here!

Jemma Yes. I know!

Sylvia And so are *you*!

Jemma Yes. I know. And I wish I wasn't ...!

Sylvia jerks her head and rolls her eyes towards the kitchen, trying to indicate a course of action. Jemma stares at her, blankly, slow to comprehend. Then she joins in with Sylvia's gyrations so that they appear like a double act on the music hall. Walter and Clive watch their antics, amazed. As Walter and Clive exchange an astonished look, Sylvia whispers to Jemma, urgently

Sylvia (*whispering*) Take Clive into the kitchen ...!

At long last, Jemma catches on and turns to the men

Jemma I've just had a wonderful idea! I'll take Clive into the kitchen. (*She grabs him by the arm and starts to drag him away*)
Walter She's doing it again!
Clive I don't want to go into the kitchen!
Jemma Yes, you do! There's something I want to show you.
Walter (*to Sylvia*) There! What did I tell you? (*He laughs*)
Clive No!
Jemma Don't be such a spoilsport, Clive. It'll be fun. You know it will. We'll have some coffee and a biscuit and a little chat, and I'll show you the freezer. (*She smiles, coquettishly*)
Walter You'd better watch out. She gets very frisky in front of the freezer.
Jemma Come on, Clive! One, two, three — hop! One, two, three — hop! One, two, three — hop!

They both go hopping out into the kitchen

Walter goes to Sylvia. She smiles, nervously

Walter So I was right — there *was* a man in here!
Sylvia Yes ... I'm afraid so ...
Walter Why did you tell me there wasn't?
Sylvia I ... I thought it might be embarrassing.
Walter For who?
Sylvia Well ... for Jemma, of course!
Walter Why should she be embarrassed?
Sylvia (*thinking hard*) Because Clive arrived here ... on the river.
Walter On the *river*?
Sylvia In a rowing boat.

Walter Ah! That's why he's wearing shorts?
Sylvia Exactly!
Walter Why?
Sylvia What?
Walter Why did he arrive on the river?
Sylvia Because he didn't want to be seen arriving at the front door!
Walter Why not?

Sylvia drifts towards the sofa

Sylvia (*improvising desperately*) Well, you see, Walter — sometimes I ... I lend this flat to ... to Jemma.
Walter What for?
Sylvia Because she hasn't anywhere else to take him.
Walter Who?
Sylvia Her lover!
Walter The one with the limp?
Sylvia Yes!

Walter explodes with laughter

Walter A lover with a limp! So *that's* what he's doing here!
Sylvia Yes.
Walter Hasn't she got a flat of her own?
Sylvia Yes. In Ponders End. But her husband's in it.
Walter So you lend your flat to Jemma to — ?
Sylvia Yes!
Walter Good heavens! I'd better have a whisky. (*He heads for the drinks cupboard*)
Sylvia (*following him in alarm*) I thought you were drinking beer.
Walter Well, I'm drinking whisky *now*! (*He laughs*)

Walter opens the drinks cupboard, reaches inside and, to his astonishment, brings out the bunch of flowers. He looks at the flowers, and then at Sylvia, puzzled. They freeze

Lights up in the kitchen

Clive But I don't want to look at the freezer!

Jemma I'll get you a coffee, then.
Clive I don't want a coffee, either! I just want to know what the hell's
going on here! (*He starts hopping towards the door*)

Jemma easily intercepts him

Jemma Oh, Clive — don't leave me!
Clive (*surprised*) What?

*Jemma locks the door and takes out the key, triumphantly. Clive gazes at
her, appalled*

What on earth are you doing?

She just smiles at him

Give me the key, please!

Jemma puts the key down her cleavage and smiles at him, seductively

Jemma Hop over here and help yourself ...

They freeze

In the sitting-room ...

Walter Why did you put my flowers in the drinks cupboard? They needed
water, not whisky!
Sylvia I ... I didn't want Jemma to see them.
Walter Why not?
Sylvia Well ... (*she moves away, sadly, below the sofa*)... *she* hasn't got
any flowers ...
Walter Didn't he bring her any?
Sylvia It is a bit difficult ... in a boat.

Walter laughs, noisily

Lights out in the sitting-room

In the kitchen ...

Clive reacts to hearing Walter's laugh next door

Clive Who *is* that out there with Sylvia?
Jemma It's Walter.
Clive I know it's Walter, but what's he doing here?
Jemma (*staring at him, blankly*) What?
Clive What's Walter doing in this flat?!
Jemma Oh, he's ... he's visiting.
Clive Visiting who?
Jemma Do you really want to know?
Clive Yes, I do!
Jemma Oh. What a pity ... (*improvising, desperately*) Well, you see, Clive ... sometimes Sylvia ... lends this flat ... er ... to *me*.
Clive To you?
Jemma Yes.
Clive What for?
Jemma Sorry?
Clive Why does Sylvia lend her flat to *you* ?!
Jemma Because I live in Ponders End.
Clive (*with a shrug*) Well?
Jemma And so does my husband.
Clive What's that got to do with Walter?
Jemma Well, I haven't anywhere else to take him.
Clive Your husband?
Jemma My lover!
Clive Your *lover*?
Jemma Don't sound so surprised. I have had lovers in my time.
Clive You mean — you borrow this flat to ...?
Jemma Yes! Oh, don't worry — he brings a book of instructions.
Clive And Walter is your ...?
Jemma Yes!
Clive Wait a minute, though! Sylvia wouldn't have lent you the flat *tonight* ...
Jemma Oh, no!
Clive So why is Walter here?
Jemma I ... I expect he got the dates mixed up!
Clive But, Jemma ... if Walter's your lover ... why is *he* out there with

Sylvia and you're in here with me with the key of the door down your cleavage?

Jemma Well, I don't want him to take me for granted, do I? (*With relish*) I wanted to make him jealous ...

Clive (*alarmed*) *I* don't want to make him jealous! (*He starts towards the door*)

Jemma Where are you going?

Clive To tell him I know all about it!

Jemma No! You mustn't!

Clive Why not?

Jemma Well, he ... he'd be embarrassed if he thought I'd told you.

Clive Yes, but —

Jemma So now you don't have to wonder about Walter, do you?

Clive No. And it's quite a relief, I can tell you! At first I thought he and Sylvia might be ... well — you know ....

Jemma Oh, no, you silly boy! Fancy thinking something like that.

Clive So *now* is it all right if we go back in there?

Jemma I hope so ...! I wonder what *they've* been talking about ...

Clive (*holding out his hand*) Key, please ...

Jemma Aren't you going to try and get it?

Clive No fear!

Jemma You are a spoilsport ... (*She looks for the key down her cleavage, but cannot find it*) It's gone!

Clive What?!

Jemma (*searching, frantically, in her bosom as before*) I can't find it!

Clive Oh, no ...!

Jemma I had it a moment ago! I think I've lost it!

Jemma pulls the front of her pyjamas away from her bosom as she did before and peers down her front, desperately. Then she looks at Clive

Don't *you* want to look?

Clive No, thank you!

Jemma All right. Please yourself ...

Jemma gets the metal tray and stands on it. She shimmies and shakes her body as before until the key falls out with a clatter on to the tray. She picks it up, triumphantly, and goes to unlock the door

Lights up in the sitting-room

Walter, still holding the bunch of flowers, reacts to the noise of the door and chuckles

Walter Ah-ha! He's trying to get out of the kitchen! I bet *I* know where she put the key ...

Jemma and Clive come in from the kitchen. Lights out in the kitchen

Jemma I've just been showing Clive the freezer.
Walter (*heavily suspicious*) You took a long time. Is that *all* you've been showing him?

Clive misunderstands Walter's attitude, and he panics

Clive Yes, that's all! There's nothing for you to be jealous about!
Walter (*puzzled*) What?

Jemma glares at Clive

Jemma Clive ...!
Sylvia (*crossing to Jemma*) Why on earth should Walter be jealous?
Jemma I'll tell you later ...!
Sylvia What?
Clive (*sitting in the armchair*) It's all right. I know all about Walter.
Sylvia Do you?
Jemma Yes, he does! (*Giving Clive another look*) But he promised not to say anything ... (*She sees Walter holding the bunch of flowers and goes to him, impulsively*) Oh, Walter — what lovely flowers! You shouldn't have bothered! (*She takes the flowers from him*)
Walter Those aren't for you! (*He takes the flowers back*)
Jemma You haven't been buying flowers for other people, have you? (*She snatches the flowers back again*)
Walter Yes, I have! (*He snatches them back*)
Jemma Oh, Walter ...!
Sylvia (*puzzled*) Jemma — could I have a word ...?
Jemma No — not now!
Walter I'm very sorry *you* haven't got any flowers, Jemma, but that's not my fault. I bought these for —

Jemma ⎫
Sylvia ⎬ (*together*) No, you didn't!

Walter What?

Jemma You bought them for me! (*She grabs the flowers again*) They're mine! (*She hugs the flowers, protectively, and rocks them in her arms like a baby*)

Walter No! I bought them for Sylvia!

A dreadful moment. Reactions

Clive For *Sylvia*?

Walter Yes, of course!

Sylvia Don't be silly, Walter! Why should you bring *me* flowers?

Walter Well, if you don't know I can't have been doing what I've been doing very well, can I?

Clive looks puzzled, and tries to understand this

Jemma (*suddenly*) Ah! Yes!

They all look at her in surprise

Sylvia What?

Jemma Why shouldn't he?

Sylvia (*puzzled by this volte-face*) What?

Jemma Why shouldn't Walter bring you flowers if he wants to?

Sylvia (*totally lost*) Well, I ... I ...

Jemma You deserve them.

Sylvia Do I?

Jemma I expect he wanted to thank you.

Sylvia Thank me for what?

Jemma For letting him use your flat to do it in. You do use this flat to do it in, don't you, Walter?

Walter Well ... yes, I do, but —

Jemma There you are, then! (*She hands to flowers to Sylvia, abruptly*) You'd better put them in water. They're beginning to wilt.

Sylvia So am I ...!

Jemma Oh, Walter, you are awful! But I'll forgive you this once. Only next time you buy flowers make sure you buy them for *me* ... (*She cuddles up to him and smiles, sexily*)

Walter stares at her, bleakly, not knowing what is going on. Clive smiles in amusement. Sylvia puts down the flowers and goes to Jemma, quickly, remembering the story she told Walter ...

Sylvia Jemma ...
Jemma *(clinging on to Walter)* Go away, Sylvia ...
Sylvia You shouldn't be embracing Walter ...
Jemma Why not? I'm enjoying myself.
Sylvia *(pointedly)* Not in front of Clive ...!

Jemma turns to look blankly at Sylvia, not knowing what Sylvia has told Walter

Jemma I beg your pardon?
Sylvia Not ... in front ... of *Clive*.
Jemma Sorry?
Sylvia You don't want to embarrass Clive, do you?
Clive I'm not embarrassed! *(He grins, broadly)*
Jemma I wish I knew what you were talking about.
Sylvia *I* wish you did, too ...!
Walter *(smiling) I* know what she's talking about.
Jemma Do you, Walter?
Walter Yes. Sylvia's been telling me all about it.
Jemma *(to Sylvia)* Have you?
Sylvia Yes!
Jemma *(to Walter)* All about what?
Walter Well ... you know ...! *(He gives her a saucy nudge, and chuckles)*
Jemma No, I don't know! And I wish I *did* know ...
Walter Sylvia told me just now.
Jemma Oh, did she? *(Aside, to Sylvia)* Well, I wish she'd told *me* ...!
Walter And I must say I'm surprised at you, Jemma.
Jemma Are you? I wonder what I've been doing ...
Walter What will they think in Ponders End? *(He laughs)*
Sylvia Walter ...!
Jemma What do *you* know about Ponders End?
Walter If only they knew ...!
Jemma Knew what?
Sylvia *(intervening, hastily)* Walter! Isn't it time you went home?

Walter No. I'm enjoying myself.

Sylvia Well, you shouldn't be!

Walter (*grinning at Jemma*) Anyway, now I know why you had your clothes off when I arrived!

Jemma Well, of course you do, Walter. I was waiting for *you*, wasn't I? (*She smiles and cuddles him closely*)

Walter looks at her in surprise. Clive smiles, delightedly. Sylvia panics and races across to Clive

Sylvia Clive! You must be exhausted after all that hopping! Let me take you into the bedroom.

Clive (*smiling, enthusiastically*) Oh, yes! What a good idea ...!

Sylvia helps him to his feet

Walter (*to Jemma*) You'd better stop her.

Jemma Why?

Walter (*playfully*) She's going to take Clive into her bedroom ...!

Jemma Oh, good! That'll leave us alone, won't it? (*She grins at him, hopefully*)

Walter Oh, my God ...! (*He escapes from her above the sofa*)

Sylvia abandons Clive and races across to Jemma

Sylvia No, Jemma!

Jemma No? I thought I was doing rather well.

Sylvia (*whispering, urgently*) Yes, you are! Much *too* well! I need to talk to you ...!

Jemma (*whispering also*) Yes — and I need to talk to *you* ...! (*She goes after Walter with a big smile*) Oh, Walter ... (*She takes his arm*)

Sylvia races back to Clive

Sylvia Clive! Come and lie down in the bedroom!

Clive Good idea ...!

They go towards the bedrooms

Anxious to escape from Jemma, Walter extricates himself and sets off after Clive

Walter I'll come and keep you company —
Clive What?!
Jemma *You* don't have to go!
Walter Oh, yes, I do ...!

Sylvia opens the door to Bedroom 2

Sylvia This way, Clive!
Clive (*cheerfully*) Right!

   He hops into Bedroom 2

Walter Wait for me!

He is about to follow, but Sylvia closes the door in his face, abruptly, as he reaches it. Jemma throws open the door to Bedroom 1

Jemma This way, Walter!
Walter (*surprised*) What?

   Jemma pushes Walter into Bedroom 1 and shuts the door

She and Sylvia shake hands. Then Sylvia leads Jemma away from the bedroom doors

Sylvia Now — there's something I've got to tell you!
Jemma Yes — and there's something *I've* got to tell *you* !

The front doorbell rings

   You're not expecting anyone *else*, are you?
Sylvia No! I ... I don't think so ... I'll see who it is.

   She goes into the hall

Jemma Probably the night shift coming on ...

Sylvia (*off*) Eddie! What are *you* doing here?

Eddie (*off*) I promised I'd do that cupboard in your spare bedroom — remember?

Eddie comes in from the hall, with Sylvia following, anxiously. Eddie is a working-class man of about thirty-five, wearing overalls and a sports jacket and carring an armful of wood and a bag of tools

Sylvia You can't do it now!

Eddie Well, I got the wood, see? So I thought I'd make a start. (*He sees Jemma*) Oh. Haven't caught you at a bad time, have I? Why are you both dressed like that? Bit early for bed, isn't it?

Eddie moves away and drops his wood and toolbag on the floor near the armchair

Sylvia Eddie! It's not convenient!

Jemma No, it certainly isn't ...!

Eddie Oh, dear. And I've come all the way from Streatham. (*To Jemma*) I expect Sylv's told you all about me?

Jemma No. She hasn't said a word ... (*She gives Sylvia a hard look*)

Eddie Oh, Sylv ...! You should have told your friend.

Sylvia I ... I must have forgotten ...

Eddie How could you forget? (*To Jemma, smiling, cheerfully*) Sylv and me are going to be married!

Jemma looks at Sylvia, appalled

Jemma Well — congratulations! What a *lovely* surprise! (*She pick up the bunch of flowers and dumps them, abruptly, into Sylvia's hands*)

The two bedroom doors open in unison, and Walter and Clive look in. They see Eddie and disappear hastily back inside, slamming the doors behind them

Eddie is astonished, and looks at Sylvia. Sylvia looks at Jemma, frantically. Jemma sinks on to the sofa in despair

Black-out

CURTAIN

ACT II

Five minutes later

Clive is sitting glumly on the sofa with his bad foot up. Walter is standing nearby, eating nuts contemplatively from a dish he is holding

From Bedroom 2 the sound of wood being sawn and an occasional tap-tap of a hammer

Quite a pause

Walter Bloody funny time for a carpenter to call.
Clive Yes ...

Pause

Walter Did you see his face when you and I popped out of the bedrooms?
Clive Yes ...

Pause

Walter He probably thought Sylvia had got two lovers!
Clive Yes!

They laugh. Walter chews his nuts. He nods towards Clive's foot

Walter How did you *get* that, anyway? (*He chuckles*) Running away from her, were you?
Clive Sorry?

Walter casts a furtive glance towards the bedrooms and then sits beside him, secretively

Walter How long's it all been going on?

Clive All what?

Walter All this ... with you two. (*He indicates the bedrooms with a jerk of his head*)

Clive (*astonished*) You *know* about us?

Walter Oh, yes.

Clive I didn't think she'd told anybody ...

Walter Well, she has.

Clive (*with a shrug*) Five months, I suppose. On and off.

Walter On and off?

Clive (*embarrassed*) We only meet once a fortnight.

Walter Good Lord. More off than on. (*He takes a mouthful of nuts*) And do you *always* arrive in a rowing boat?

Clive Yes. A mile and a half from the boathouse in my shorts ...

Walter (*eating*) Have you never thought of arriving fully-clothed at the front door?

Clive She prefers the river. Says it's more ... romantic.

Walter Sounds kinky to me. And afterwards?

Clive I row back again.

Walter I'm surprised you've got the strength!

Clive (*gloomily*) I won't be tonight, though ...

Walter Sorry?

Clive Rowing back. My boat's disappeared. Slipped its moorings and drifted off.

Walter And you've left your clothes a mile and a half up the river in the boathouse?

Clive Yes ...!

Walter laughs

The door to Bedroom 2 opens and Sylvia comes bursting out anxiously. They both look at her in surprise. She smiles nervously and crosses below them, trying to appear nonchalant

Sylvia Well! Fancy the carpenter turning up out of the blue like that!

The men exchange a look

Walter You weren't expecting him, then?

Sylvia Not tonight!

Walter What?

Sylvia Not today!

Clive Then why don't you tell him to go away and come back tomorrow?

Sylvia That's what I've been doing! But he won't ...

Walter Well, I hope you're not paying him overtime.

Sylvia (*anxiously*) Where's Jemma?

Clive She went into the kitchen.

Walter She always does! (*He and Clive laugh*)

Sylvia What's she doing in the kitchen?

Walter Getting herself a cup of coffee.

Sylvia I hope you two haven't been talking to each other ...

Clive (*glaring at her*) Yes, we have!

Sylvia Have you?

Walter Oh, yes. We've been having a very interesting conversation as a matter of fact ...

Sylvia Oh, dear ...!

Jemma comes in from the kitchen with a mug of coffee. Sylvia goes to her, urgently

Where have you been?

Jemma (*giving her a hard look*) After what I've heard tonight I needed a cup of coffee!

Sylvia This is no time for coffee!

Jemma Oh, yes, it is! I don't want to fall asleep, do I? I might miss something exciting.

Sylvia I left you in here talking to Walter! *Clive's* not supposed to be talking to Walter!

Clive Why not?

Sylvia Er ... well ... you're supposed to be resting your foot.

Clive That doesn't stop me talking to Walter. (*He looks at Walter and shrugs*)

Sylvia (*whispering to Jemma, urgently*) Get Walter into the kitchen ...!

Jemma *Again?*

Sylvia hastens to the bedroom doors and turns to the men with a sweet smile

Sylvia I'm just going to put my clothes on.

Clive What for?

Sylvia Well, I can't wander about in my dressing-gown with the carpenter here, can I?

Walter Why not? It was good enough for the plumber and the window-cleaner. (*He laughs*)

Sylvia stumbles out into Bedroom 1, slamming the door behind her

Jemma sips her coffee, uncertainly

Jemma Well, what a funny time for a carpenter to call!

Walter Yes. I think we're all agreed on that.

Jemma *I* can't even find one during working hours, never mind in the evening. Sylvia must have a special way of handling them. (*She puts down her coffee, grabs Walter and pulls him towards the kitchen*)

Walter What the hell are you doing?

Jemma *You*'re going into the kitchen!

Walter What for?

Jemma To look at the freezer.

Walter I've seen it already!

Jemma (*hopefully*) Tumble dryer?

Walter No, thanks!

Jemma Well, you can't stay in here!

Walter Why not? (*Then he realizes*) Ah. No. Of course not. Sorry. You two want to be alone.

Clive No, we *don't*!

Jemma Come on, Walter!

She drags Walter into the kitchen. Clive watches them go, astonished

Lights up in the kitchen. Jemma pulls Walter in, slams the door shut and leans against it, a trifle breathless

Jemma Now — you stay in *here*!

Walter Why don't you take Clive into one of the bedrooms?

Jemma (*puzzled*) I beg your pardon?

Walter Instead of making me sit out here in the kitchen while you carry on in the sitting-room ...

Jemma What are you talking about?

Walter Oh, come on! You don't have to pretend. I know all about it.

Jemma Well, that's more than I do! (*She starts to go*)

Walter Let me know when it's all clear.

Jemma What?

Walter Out there!

Jemma (*bemused*) Oh. Right.

She hastens out. Walter settles with his whisky to wait

In the sitting-room ...

Clive looks up as Jemma returns. She marches purposefully towards the bedrooms

Clive *Now* where are you off to?

Jemma I'm going to put my clothes on.

Clive (*with a grin*) Aren't you going to stay in the kitchen with Walter?

Jemma No fear!

Clive I thought you *wanted* to be with Walter.

Jemma What? (*She remembers her story*) Oh — yes! I do, don't I? I'd forgotten that. But I think I'll put my clothes on first.

Clive It was hardly worth your while taking them off, was it?

Jemma Well, *I* didn't know the carpenter was going to call!

Eddie comes out of Bedroom 2

Jemma leaps into his path and extends her arms to prevent his approach

No! You can't come in!

Eddie brushes her aside and moves past her into the room, heavy with suspicion

Eddie I've been thinking while I was in there. There's something untoward going on here tonight, if you want my opinion ...

Jemma I don't know what you're talking about!

Eddie I'm talking about two men popping out of two bedrooms! (*He glares at Clive*)

Clive What's it got to do with you?

Jemma (*to Eddie*) I can explain that — !

Eddie And can you explain why you and Sylv both had your clothes off at half-past seven?

Jemma We were going to have an early night.

Eddie With two blokes in the flat?!

Jemma Well, Walter wasn't supposed to be here ...

Eddie What were you going to do, then? Share this one between the two of you?

Jemma Don't be vulgar!

Clive It's none of your business if they were!

Eddie (*glaring at Clive*) And where are your trousers?

Clive A mile and a half up the river ...

Eddie What?!

Jemma He always arrives without any trousers.

Eddie I think I'd better have a word with Sylv ...

He starts to go towards Bedroom 1. Jemma intercepts him, her arms outstretched again

Jemma You can't go in there!

Eddie Why not?

Jemma She's putting her clothes back on.

Eddie About time, too! Well, as soon as she's finished, I've got some questions for her! (*He goes towards the kitchen*)

Jemma races around and intercepts him again, her arms outstretched once more

Jemma You can't go in there!

Eddie (*wearily*) Will you stop doing that? I'm only going to look for a dustpan and brush.

He pushes her aside and goes through into the kitchen. Jemma smiles, nervously, at Clive

Jemma He's very friendly for a carpenter, isn't he?

Clive A damn sight *too* friendly, if you ask me!

Jemma hovers near the kitchen door, angling her body towards it so that she can hear what is being said inside. Clive watches her in surprise

In the kitchen ...

Walter looks up as Eddie comes in

Walter Ah. You finished, then?
Eddie Finished? I've hardly started. Just come for a dustpan.
Walter Over there.

Eddie peers at Walter suspiciously

Eddie You a *friend* of Sylvia's?
Walter Well, I don't usually call on total strangers and sit down in their kitchens.

Eddie peers more closely at Walter

Eddie What's going on here?
Walter You're building a cupboard and I'm sitting down in the kitchen.

In the sitting-room, Jemma presses her ear to the door, trying to hear

Eddie You think I'm daft or something? I ask you! What am *I* supposed to think?
Walter If I were you I should concentrate on carpentry.
Eddie Two men coming out of two bedrooms!
Walter Well, that's better than two men coming out of *one* bedroom.
Eddie And one without his trousers on! Who are you, anyhow?
Walter I don't see that it's any of your business, but if you must know —

Jemma comes hurtling in from the sitting-room. Walter and Eddie look at her in surprise

Jemma (*to Eddie*) You can't stay in here!
Eddie Are you off your trolley?
Walter He's looking for a dustpan.

Jemma races to where the dustpan lives, picks it up, returns to Eddie and thrusts it into his hands

Jemma There you are! Off you go now! Don't hang about! (*She urges him on his way*)

Eddie But I want to know who he is and what ——

Jemma You can't stay in here!

Eddie Why not?

Jemma (*who does not know*) Why not?! Well ... because ... (*with sudden inspiration*) because poor old Walter's not very well.

Walter What?!

Jemma (*lowering her voice, sadly*) High blood pressure. He mustn't get over-excited. That's why he's sitting down all on his own in the kitchen ...

Walter It is *not!*

Jemma Oh, Walter, you don't have to pretend. It's nothing to be ashamed of. It might happen to anyone.

Walter Don't pay any attention to her!

Jemma Now remember what the doctor said. You mustn't get so excited. (*She clasps his head to her bosom and rocks it gently like a baby*) There, there ...

Eddie (*sympathetically*) Oh, dear — I ... I didn't know that. (*Whispering*) Sorry if I made a bit of a noise. Poor old man. You'd better rest. (*He starts to tiptoe away*)

Walter (*emerging*) I am not an old man and there's nothing wrong with me!

Jemma pulls his face back into her bosom, abruptly

Jemma Oh, yes, there is! (*She rocks his head again*) There, there ...

Eddie So *that's* what you're doing here, then? You're looking after Walter.

Walter (*emerging again*) No, she isn't!

Jemma pulls his face firmly back into her bosom

Jemma Yes, that's right! I'm the District Nurse.

Walter (*muffled*) What?!

He tries to escape, but Jemma clings on to his head, firmly. Eddie nods to her, knowingly

Eddie Well, in that case I'd case I'd better leave you with your patient.

Walter surfaces again

Walter Don't believe a word she says!
Jemma (*soothingly*) You mustn't keep talking to people. You're supposed to be resting, not talking to people. (*She goes to Eddie, urgently*) Off you go, then! (*She opens the door*) Sylvia's not paying you to stand about talking to invalids.

Jemma pushes him out through the doorway so abruptly that he nearly loses his balance. She turns to Walter, who is approaching at speed

You stay here!

She goes out and shuts the door in Walter's face. He looks puzzled, bends down and peers through the keyhole

In the sitting-room ...

Clive looks astonished as Eddie comes flying out of the kitchen, followed by Jemma. She pushes Eddie to Bedroom 2, opens the door, shoves him inside unceremoniously, and turns to smile at Clive, innocently

He's supposed to be making a cupboard.

She goes into Bedroom 2 after Eddie, shuts the door, then reappears immediately

I'm only going in there to get my clothes. (*She starts to go again, then hesitates*) I do hope the carpenter hasn't got sawdust all over them. (*She disappears and shuts the door*)

Walter looks in from the kitchen

Walter Has she gone?
Clive I think so.

Walter ambles in. Lights out in the kitchen

Walter I hope you know what you're letting yourself in for.
Clive Sorry?
Walter You're not really serious, are you?
Clive Serious?
Walter About *her*. (*He indicates the bedrooms*)
Clive Of course I'm serious. I want to marry her.
Walter Good Lord! I'd better get you a drink. (*He heads for the drinks cupboard*) G and T?
Clive Fine.

Walter pours their drinks

Anyway ... what about *you*?
Walter I'm having whisky.
Clive I mean you and ... *yours*.
Walter Sorry?
Clive (*indicating the bedrooms*) Out there.
Walter (*astonished*) You *know* about us?
Clive Oh, yes.
Walter I didn't think she'd told anybody ...
Clive Well, she has.
Walter Good Lord ... (*He returns with the drinks*)
Clive Thanks. How often do you meet yours?
Walter (*sheepishly*) Well, if you must know ... once a fortnight.
Clive Same as us! And are your intentions strictly honourable about yours?
Walter Certainly. I want to marry her.

Clive has a splendid idea

Clive I say! Perhaps we could have a double wedding?

They both laugh at the prospect, clink their glasses and drink each other's health

The door to Bedroom 1 bursts open and Sylvia comes racing in. She is now dressed. She reacts in alarm at seeing the men together

Sylvia Walter! You should be in the kitchen!

The door to Bedroom 2 bursts open and Jemma comes out with an armful of clothes and makes for Bedroom 1

Jemma!

Jemma stops, and they whisper to each other, urgently

Sylvia You were supposed to take Walter into the kitchen!
Jemma I did!
Sylvia Well, he's out again!
Jemma (*seeing Walter*) Oh, my God — so he is ...! Well, *you* can do it this time! I'm going to get my clothes on before any *more* men arrive!

She glares at Sylvia and darts out into Bedroom 1, slamming the door behind her

Sylvia hastens to Walter, anxious to be rid of him

Sylvia Come along, Walter. Into the kitchen ...
Walter No point in my going into the kitchen if Jemma isn't there. Is there, Clive? (*He winks at him*)
Sylvia What are you talking about?
Walter How long have you known the carpenter?
Sylvia Er ... not very long. Why?
Walter He was asking a lot of questions. Wanted to know what was going on here.
Sylvia (*alarmed*) You didn't tell him, did you?
Walter Certainly not!
Sylvia Thank God for that ...!
Walter Did you see his face when Clive and I appeared out of the bedrooms?
Sylvia Yes, I did! And I don't know *how* I'm going to explain it to him. He must have wondered what you were both doing here ...
Walter None of his damn business! Any more nuts? (*He wanders out into the kitchen*)
Clive Why did you go and tell *him* about us? I thought it was our little secret.

Sylvia Well, I ... I had to tell him *something.*
Clive Why?
Sylvia Because he ... he might have wondered what *you* were doing here.

Walter returns with a fresh supply of nuts

Clive *Did* you, Walter?
Walter *(intent on his nuts)* What?
Clive Wonder what I was doing here.
Walter Yes. I did, as a matter of fact. I'm not used to seeing strange men hopping about in shorts. *(He ambles towards the balcony)*
Sylvia *(following him, anxiously)* But, Walter — you *know* what he's doing here!
Walter Yes. I do *now.* And I must say it's a pity you can't let him have it more than once a fortnight.
Sylvia *(confused)* Sorry?
Walter The flat!
Sylvia Oh. Yes. Of course.
Clive *(with a grin)* And in future, Walter — no turning up here unexpectedly, eh?
Walter Sorry about that, old boy. But I didn't know about *you,* then, did I?

He chuckles and wanders out on to the balcony with his nuts and looks down at the view of the river. Sylvia returns to Clive and hovers, nervously

Sylvia I ... I suppose *you* must be wondering what *Walter's* doing here ...
Clive *(casually)* No.
Sylvia You're *not?*
Clive I know what he's doing here.
Sylvia You do?!
Clive Yes. It's just a pity he came barging in on *my* night.

Sylvia considers this for a second, then races out to Walter and whispers, urgently

Sylvia You didn't tell *Clive* what you came here for, did you?
Walter I didn't have to. You'd already told him.

Sylvia No, I hadn't!
Walter Well, he knows.
Sylvia About us?
Walter Yes.
Sylvia Oh, my God ...!
Walter Why? Doesn't matter, does it?
Sylvia Ah — no — no, of course not!

She laughs, nervously, and runs back inside to Clive and seethes a little

    Clive ...
Clive Yes?
Sylvia Is it true?
Clive What?
Sylvia That you don't mind about what Walter's doing here.
Clive Why should *I* mind? It's none of my business what Walter does in
    his spare time. I just don't want him doing it on the same night as me.
Sylvia What?!

*Sylvia is about to explode at this apparent insensitivity, but Walter
wanders back in from the balcony*

    Clive! That ankle must be so painful! Why don't you go and lie down
    in the spare room?
Clive I can't ! The bloody plumber's in there!
Sylvia Well, use *my* room, then!
Walter He can't do that! What would Jemma say? (*He laughs, noisily*)
Clive What?

Jemma comes in from Bedroom 1. She is now dressed again

Jemma There! That didn't take long, did it?
Walter (*grinning*) Well, you have had plenty of practice, haven't you?
Jemma Practice?
Walter At taking your clothes off and putting them on again in a hurry!
    (*He laughs*)

Jemma remembers the story she has told Clive and smiles, coyly, at Walter

Jemma Oh, Walter! You don't have to *tell* everyone ...! (*She gives him a saucy push and hastens across to Sylvia*)

Walter's smile fades and he looks at Clive, puzzled. Clive smiles back at him, happily. Sylvia is out of her depth, and panics

Sylvia Now you boys really must go home! Poor Jemma's had a long journey and she wants to go to bed.

Walter And take her clothes off again? She's only just put them on! (*He and Clive laugh*)

Sylvia Walter, there's no point in your staying here. There can't be any conversation now that the carpenter's called.

Jemma (*quietly*) I don't think conversation's what they came here for ...!

Sylvia gives her a look

Clive Yes, you go home, Walter. After all, fair's fair, it wasn't your night tonight. So why don't you drive Jemma back to Ponders End?

Walter No fear!

Clive It's all right. You can drop her outside. Her husband won't see you. He'll think she's arrived in a taxi.

Jemma I don't want to go to Ponders End!

Walter No. I expect *you* want to go to Venice.

Jemma Why should I go to Venice?

Walter Well, *every*one travels by boat in Venice! (*He grins at her, and starts to sing*) "Just one Cornetto ...!"

Jemma turns to Sylvia, bewildered

Jemma What *is* he talking about?

Sylvia (*quietly*) I'll tell you when they've gone ...! Walter, you really must go! This flat is far too full.

Jemma Especially now the carpenter's called. Life's full of surprises, isn't it?

Clive It certainly is! Fancy you coming back from France and finding dear old Walter waiting for you.

Sylvia, puzzled, turns to Jemma, who smiles, innocently

Sylvia I didn't know dear old Walter *was* waiting for you ...

Walter Neither did dear old Walter!
Clive (*to Walter*) Of course you were!
Jemma (*to Sylvia*) Of course he was!
Sylvia What?

Jemma nods, frantically

Walter Why on earth should I be waiting for Jemma?
Clive Oh, come on! You don't have to pretend. We all know what you
came here for. Don't we, Jemma?

So Jemma has to hastily act up to Walter again ...

Jemma Of course we do! Don't be so shy, Walter!

*She giggles girlishly; pushes him playfully; puts a flower between her
teeth and dances; pushes him again; covers her face with her hands, coyly;
etc. Walter and Sylvia watch her performance in astonishment. Clive smiles,
enjoying it enormously. Finally Jemma runs out of steam and sinks onto
the sofa, exhausted*

Walter (*to Jemma*) Have you gone mad?
Sylvia I can't think what this is all about ...
Clive About your flat, of course.
Sylvia What's my flat got to do with Jemma behaving like that?
Clive Well, she can hardly carry on her love life in Ponders End with her
husband there, can she?
Walter And it's jolly nice of you to lend her your place. Even if it is only
once a fortnight! (*He and Clive laugh*)
Sylvia Jemma ... could I have a word ...?
Jemma Yes, I think you'd better! (*To the men*) We're just going into the
kitchen for a minute. (*She crosses to Sylvia*)
Walter (*to Clive*) She's off again! (*They laugh*)
Sylvia (*to Jemma, quietly*) No!
Jemma What?
Sylvia (*whispering, urgently*) We can't leave them alone! They'll talk to
each other!
Jemma Ah. Yes. Right. (*She turns back to the men*) Walter — would you
go and see if there's any sign of Clive's boat?
Walter I thought it had been carried away by the tide? It'll hardly have
turned itself round and come back again!

Jemma You never know. On a night like this *anything* could happen ...

Walter Anyway, I'm hungry ...

Sylvia You had some bread and cheese.

Walter I'd hardly call that a square meal.

Clive Well, why don't you take her out to dinner? She must be starving by now.

Walter What a good idea! Come on, Sylvia. I'll take you out to dinner.

Clive looks surprised. Jemma and Sylvia exchange a frantic look

Clive Not Sylvia — Jemma!

Jemma Oh, lovely! I'm dying for dinner.

Walter Why should I take Jemma out for dinner?

Clive (*grinning*) I should think it's the least you can do for her after what she does for you!

Sylvia Jemma ...?

Jemma smiles and shrugs, woman-of-the-world

Walter What the hell does Jemma do for *me*?

Jemma Oh, Walter! Don't tell me you've forgotten already?

Walter tries to recall

Sylvia What *do* you do for him?

Jemma Don't pretend you don't know about it!

Sylvia I *don't* know about it ...!

Jemma Don't be silly, Sylvia. Of course you do!

Sylvia Do I?

Jemma Yes! (*She nods, vigorously*)

Sylvia goes to Walter, urgently

Sylvia Walter, would you go into the kitchen for a minute?

Walter I've been there twicc already!

Sylvia (*taking him towards the kitchen*) You can make some sandwiches. You said you were hungry.

Walter I'm not very good at sandwiches ...

Sylvia Well, now's the time to learn!

Sylvia pushes Walter out into the kitchen and closes the door. He disappears out of sight into the back of the kitchen. Jemma darts across to Clive

Jemma Come on, Clive! *You* can go into the spare room! (*She pulls him to his feet*)
Sylvia No, he can't!
Jemma Why not?
Sylvia The carpenter!
Jemma Oh, yes ... (*To Clive*) Right! On to the balcony! (*She urges him on his way*)
Clive What for?
Jemma The fresh air will do you good.

She propels him out on to the balcony and closes the glass door. Clive looks back in, despondently. Jemma hastens back to Sylvia, glaring at her, furiously

Jemma You never told me you had *three* men on the go!
Sylvia (*defensively*) I didn't say *how* many there were ...

Jemma stares at her in horror

Jemma You ... you mean there might be more? Hiding?

Jemma races about, searching for men behind various bits of furniture, with Sylvia following in her wake, protesting. Outside, Clive watches the scene in astonishment. Jemma sees him. She waves. He waves back, shakes his head in disbelief and turns away to look down at the river

Sylvia (*laughing*) Jemma! Jemma! Don't be silly! Of course there aren't any more!
Jemma Are you sure?
Sylvia Yes!
Jemma Just three?
Sylvia Yes!
Jemma (*incredulously*) And you're having all of them? On approval?
Sylvia Only because I'm not sure which of them I want to marry ...

Jemma If they find out what's been going on here, you won't be marrying *any* of them!

Sylvia Why not?

Jemma Because they'll murder each other, that's why not!

Sylvia (*a bit put out*) I don't know about that. Clive didn't seem to *mind* about Walter and me ...

Jemma He doesn't know about Walter and you.

Sylvia He *said* he did. And when I asked Walter if *he* told him, he said Clive already knew.

Jemma Oh, yes — he knows all right! But not about Walter and *you*. He knows about Walter and *me*.

Sylvia What?!

Jemma Well, I had to tell him something, didn't I? We couldn't just stand there staring at the freezer. So I told Clive that Walter and I were lovers, and that you lent me your flat to do it in.

Sylvia So *that*'s what you were talking about ...!

Jemma I thought it was rather clever of me.

Sylvia Well, I hope they don't compare notes.

Jemma Why?

Sylvia Because I told Walter that you and *Clive* were lovers.

Jemma Good heavens! It looks as if I'm going to have my hands full!

Eddie comes in from Bedroom 2. He sees the girls fully clothed

Eddie Ah! You've got your clothes back on, then? About time, too.

Sylvia goes to him, smiling, hopefully

Sylvia Have you finished the cupboard already?

Eddie Finished? I've had too much on my mind, haven't I?

Sylvia Well, I wish you'd leave it till tomorrow ...

Eddie You trying to get rid of me?

Jemma Yes ...!

Eddie What?

Sylvia (*glaring at Jemma*) No, of course not!

Jemma Oh. Sorry. I thought we *were* ...

Sylvia It's just that ... all that banging ... it'll disturb the neighbours. Couldn't you come back and do it tomorrow?

Jemma Yes. You can bang away to your heart's content tomorrow.

Eddie hesitates, then relents

Eddie Oh — all right, then.

Sylvia }
Jemma } *(together)* Oh, good!

Eddie So now I can sit down here and have a nice little gossip with you girls, can't I? *(He settles himself on the sofa)*

Sylvia }
Jemma } *(together)* Oh, God!

Eddie stares for a while at Jemma. She shifts, apprehensively. He grins at her, amiably

Eddie Not wearing your uniform today, then?

Sylvia looks across at Jemma, totally bewildered. Jemma smiles, innocently

Sylvia Uniform?

Eddie Yes. I thought she'd be in uniform.

Sylvia Really?

Eddie *(to Jemma)* But you're not, are you?

Jemma No. No, I ... I'm not. I prefer to travel in mufti.

Eddie Even when you're on the job?

Jemma Oh, yes. I find it less distracting.

Eddie Well, if you were coming to visit *me*, I'd prefer to have you in a uniform.

Jemma I'll remember that ...!

Eddie I mean — if you're in uniform there's no doubt what you've come for, is there?

Jemma No, I suppose not ...

Sylvia Jemma ...?

Jemma Hmm?

Sylvia Is ... is there something I don't know about you?

Jemma goes to Sylvia, nodding, desperately

Jemma Yes, there is! I'll tell you later ...!

Eddie Is he all right now?
Jemma Sorry?
Eddie The bloke in the kitchen. Not getting over-excited, I hope?

Sylvia looks at Jemma, bewildered

Jemma Oh, no. No. I ... I think he's got himself under control now.
Sylvia I hope so! He's supposed to be making sandwiches.
Eddie How about the other one?
Jemma What other one?
Eddie The one with the foot!
Jemma Oh, he's out there.

Eddie gets up and looks towards the balcony, where Clive is gazing at the river

Eddie He shouldn't be standing outside, should he?
Jemma Oh, I think the fresh air will do him good.
Eddie Ah, well — you know best, eh? (*He grins at her, confidently*)
Sylvia (*to Jemma*) Do you?
Jemma Yes, I do!
Eddie Well, she is the expert, isn't she?
Sylvia Is she?
Jemma Yes, I am! Thank you, Eddie. It's nice to be appreciated.
Eddie (*going to Sylvia*) You should have told me what those two blokes came here for, Sylv. You'll never guess what *I* was thinking!
Jemma (*quietly*) I bet we will ...! (*She escapes away below the sofa*)
Eddie You should have told me right away.
Sylvia Told you what?
Eddie That they've both come here for the treatment.

Sylvia looks across at Jemma, who smiles and shrugs, helplessly

How long has your friend been doing all this, then?

Sylvia considers this

Sylvia Doing all what?
Eddie Looking after the sick and needy.

Sylvia looks at Jemma again. Jemma gives a martyr's smile

Jemma (*with a deep sigh*) It's my way of helping those less fortunate than myself ...

Eddie But that's not what *I* came here for, is it, Sylv? (*He tries to embrace her*)

Sylvia (*escaping*) No! *You* came to build a cupboard!

Eddie You don't have to pretend. Your friend knows what I've really come here for. Don't you?

Jemma I've got a pretty rough idea ...!

Eddie (*adoringly*) Oh, Sylv ... (*He grabs her, suddenly, in a bearlike embrace*)

Sylvia (*appalled*) Eddie! (*She breaks free*) Not in front of Jemma!

Jemma Oh, don't worry about me. I'm getting more and more broadminded every minute.

Eddie (*to Sylvia*) There you are! (*He tries again*)

Sylvia No! There are ... *other* people about! (*She escapes away to Jemma*) Clive's out on the balcony ...!

Jemma glances towards the balcony. Clive is gazing out across the river, one hand up to shield his eyes

Jemma It's all right. I think he's looking for the Spanish Armada.

Eddie tries once more

Sylvia No, Eddie! Not in front of Clive! I'd be so ... embarrassed.

Eddie Let's go into the bedroom, then! (*He tries to pull her around the end of the sofa*)

Sylvia No! Jemma! Will you please help!

Jemma I don't think he needs any help.

Sylvia (*glaring at her*) You know what I mean!

Jemma Well, it's all your own fault. You shouldn't fraternize with a whole football team.

Sylvia Suppose Clive comes in?

Outside, Clive turns from his search for the Armada and looks into the room

Eddie Oh, come on, Sylv! Don't hang about!

Eddie pulls Sylvia around the end of the sofa so abruptly that she almost loses her footing. Clive cannot believe his eyes

Sylvia (*resisting*) No! Certainly not!

Sylvia and Eddie struggle. Clive comes nearer to the window to get a better look. Jemma sees him and hastily gets between him and the struggling pair. She executes a desperate dance with much flailing of arms, trying to distract Clive's attention. Clive watches the incredible scene for a few moments, then slides the glass door open and hops inside

Clive What the hell's going on?

Jemma We're rehearsing for the office pantomime.

Clive (*going to Sylvia*) Are you all right?

Sylvia Yes — yes, of course!

Clive (*glaring at Eddie*) What did you think you were doing?

Eddie What's that got to do with you?

Jemma He was only trying to show her his cupboard.

Clive I wondered what he was trying to show her!

Eddie Now, now — you mustn't get agitated ...

Clive Why not?

Eddie (*to Jemma*) I told you he shouldn't have been standing up. You'd better take him into the bedroom and put him under sedation.

Jemma Good idea! Come on, Clive! Let's go into the bedroom.

Clive I'm not going in there with you!

Eddie Don't be daft. That's what she came here for!

Clive What?! (*He looks at Jemma in surprise*)

Jemma (*acting as Florence Nightingale*) Yes. I'm here to tend to your every need ...

Clive Not *my* need — Walter's!

Eddie (*to Jemma*) You can manage two of 'em, can't you?

Jemma (*modestly*) Well, I'll do my best ...

Eddie You must have had plenty of practice.

Jemma Not lately ...! (*She grins at Sylvia*)

Eddie When you were training I bet you could handle half a dozen at a time!

Jemma Yes, but I was younger then ...

Walter comes in from the kitchen wearing an apron

Walter What do you fancy? Cucumber or tomato?

They all look at him, blankly, for a moment

Sylvia What are you talking about?
Walter I thought you wanted some sandwiches. (*He sees Eddie and grunts his disapproval*) Oh — *you're* still here, then?
Clive Yes, and he doesn't seem to be able to keep his mind on the job! (*He glares at Eddie*)
Jemma (*quietly*) I thought that's what he *had* been doing ...
Clive If I hadn't come in when I did he'd probably have dragged Sylvia into the bedroom.
Walter What?!

Eddie goes to Walter, solicitously

Eddie Now don't you go getting yourself all agitated again. Remember your blood pressure.
Walter There's nothing wrong with my blood pressure!
Eddie Ssh! Ssh! Gently, now ... You come and sit down. (*To Jemma, appealing for help*) Nurse!
Sylvia }
Clive } (*together*) Nurse?!

Jemma goes quickly to assist Eddie

Jemma Yes, Walter — you mustn't get over-excited.
Walter Don't start all that again!
Jemma Why don't you come with me and have a lie-down in the bedroom?
Walter Are you sex-mad or something?
Jemma I was, but I'm a bit out of practice.
Eddie We tried to get *Clive* to go into the bedroom with her, but he wouldn't.
Walter (*to Clive*) Why not?

Clive looks puzzled

Clive Well, I ... I didn't think you'd like me to ...

Walter Nothing to do with *me*.

Jemma No — he's very broadminded.

Walter I'd be delighted!

Clive Would you?

Walter Of course.

Clive (*in disbelief*) You ... you wouldn't *mind* my going into the bedroom with Jemma?

Walter (*laughing*) Well, if *you* don't mind, *I* certainly don't!

Clive But I thought you and Jemma were — ?

Sylvia
Jemma } (*together*) Aaah!

The men all look at them in surprise

Jemma (*desperately*) Do come and have a lie-down, Walter!

Walter No fear!

Eddie You don't have to worry. She's quite an expert.

Jemma Yes. I've been doing it for years.

Eddie She ought to have both of you lying down by rights.

Walter Both of us?!

Eddie Yes.

Jemma Come on, Walter!

Walter Not likely!

Eddie (*to Jemma*) Well, if he won't lie down in there, we'd better put him on the sofa.

Jemma Good idea!

Jemma and Eddie each take one of Walter's arms and lead him across to the sofa. They plonk him down, abruptly

Walter What the hell do you think you're doing?

Jemma gets a rug from the chest and wraps it expertly around his knees. Everyone looks dumbfounded. Jemma peels a banana, nonchalantly. Walter finally recovers his power of speech

Now look here — I think there's something this carpenter ought to know!

Jemma shoves the peeled banana into his mouth. The others all look aghast. Freeze the picture. Finally, Walter removes the banana from his mouth, outraged

Have you gone mad?

Jemma You said you were hungry.

Walter Well, you don't have to force-feed me!

Eddie She was only trying to help you. After all, that's what she's here for, isn't it?

Walter What are you talking about?

Eddie Jemma! She's here to look after you.

Walter Oh, no, she's not!

Clive (*reasonably*) Well ... she is in a way, Walter.

Walter looks at him, bleakly, for a moment

Walter What?

Clive Well ... you know. (*He smiles, secretively*)

Walter is puzzled

Eddie *And* you, too, Clive.

Clive Sorry?

Eddie Jemma's here for your benefit, as well.

Clive She is not!

Jemma Yes, I am!

Clive What?

Jemma (*Florence Nightingale again*) I'm here to ... to tend to your every need ...

Eddie Yes! Yours *and* Walter's.

Clive Now, hang on a bit!

Sylvia Eddie! You were supposed to be making a cupboard!

Jemma (*to Walter*) And you were supposed to be making sandwiches!

Walter That's all very well, but ——

Jemma We're all very hungry! I know I'm starving ... So we're going to need lots of sandwiches — aren't we, Sylvia?

Sylvia Yes! (*ad libbing, desperately*) I — I promised to make some for the Boy Scouts!

Jemma looks at her, checked for a moment, and giggles

Jemma *What?*
Sylvia (*losing heart*) I thought it was a good idea ...
Jemma (*incredulously*) Boy Scouts?
Sylvia For their fête?
Jemma Ah! Yes! That *is* a good idea! I wish *I'd* thought of that ...
Sylvia Which do you think they'd prefer? Cucumber or tomato?
Jemma Oh ... cucumber, I think.
Sylvia Yes. We don't them dropping tomato down their toggles, do we?
    (*She and Jemma laugh*)
Clive What the hell is this all about?
Eddie It's about your foot and his blood pressure!
Clive Sorry?
Eddie (*indicating Jemma*) Well, that's what this lady's here for, isn't it?
Clive (*puzzled*) Is it?
Eddie (*impatiently*) Yes — she's the District Nurse!

A dreadful silence. Walter starts to laugh

Walter Good Lord! You didn't *believe* what she told you in there, did
    you?
Eddie Why not?
Walter Take my word for it. Never trust Jemma when she's in the kitchen.

Eddie looks at Jemma. She smiles, nervously

Eddie You're ... *not* a nurse?

*Jemma tries to reply, opening and closing her mouth like a goldfish, but
no sound emanates so she finishes off the banana*

Walter Of course she's not a nurse! She's Sylvia's partner in the dress
    shop.

Jemma recovers her voice

Jemma Well, I was *trained* in First Aid.

Eddie Where?

Jemma The Brownies.

Eddie But if you're not the District Nurse ... and you aren't looking after the sick and needy ... what the hell are these two blokes doing here?

Sylvia (*desperately*) Eddie — there's something I must talk to you about! (*She pulls at his arm*)

Eddie Hang on a minute!

Sylvia Will you *please* come into the bedroom!

Eddie smiles delightedly, getting his priorities right

Eddie Oh, Sylv! I thought you'd never ask ...

Sylvia casts a hectic look to Jemma and then takes Eddie into Bedroom 2, closing the door after them

Walter starts to fold up the rug that was around his knees, looks at Jemma and shakes his head

Walter I'm beginning to wonder about you.

Jemma I'm beginning to wonder about myself! I could have been back home in Ponders End by now ...

Walter Well, *I'm* ready for another whisky. (*He puts the folded rug down and goes to the drinks cupboard*)

Clive looks between Walter and Jemma, and winks at her, knowingly. She looks surprised

Clive I'll leave you to it, then.

He hops towards Bedroom 2, but Jemma races around to intercept him

Jemma Where are you going?

Clive looks across at Walter, who has his back to them as he pours his whisky

Clive (*to Jemma; conspiratorily*) Don't you *want* to get rid of me?

Jemma (*blankly*) Sorry?

Clive I thought you two would want to be alone ...
Jemma Which two?
Clive You two! (*He indicates Walter's back*)

Jemma looks, and remembers

Jemma Oh! Yes! That's right! We do, don't we? I keep forgetting ...
Clive Off you go, then ...!

He gives her a firm push. The impetus carries her around in a neat circle back to him

Jemma No! I couldn't!
Clive (*a little louder*) What did you come here for, then?

Walter hears this as he turns from the drinks cupboard with his whisky

Walter *I* know what she came here for! (*He chuckles, and sips his whisky*)
Jemma (*acting shy*) Yes, Walter — but you don't have to talk about it to all and sundry. Why can't you be more romantic?
Walter Oh. Yes. Sorry. (*He winks at her*) I'll go back into the kitchen. (*He puts down his drink on the coffee table and goes towards the kitchen*)

Clive is alarmed at the prospect of being left with Jemma, and hops quickly to Walter

Clive You don't have to go!
Walter Yes, I do. If we've got all these Boy Scouts turning up somebody had better start seeing to the sandwiches.
Clive I'll help you!
Walter Don't be daft ...
Clive What?
Walter (*whispering*) I'm being tactful ...
Clive What?
Walter I'm leaving you alone with Jemma ...
Clive What for?

In despair, Walter looks across at Jemma

Walter Jemma — you do *want* to be alone with Clive, don't you?

Jemma Do I? (*She remembers*) Oh — yes — that's right! I do! I keep forgetting ...

She hastens to the astonished Clive, takes his arm and leads him towards the sofa, smiling, seductively

You come and sit down here with me ... (*She pulls him down on to the sofa beside her*)

Walter That's more like it! (*He turns to go*)

Clive (*whispering to Jemma*) You told me it was *Walter* you wanted to be alone with!

Jemma Did I? (*She remembers*) Oh — yes — that's right! I do! (*She gets up and runs across to Walter*) Oh, Walter ...!

Walter turns in surprise

Walter What?!

Jemma (*taking his arm, romantically*) Oh, Walter — *Walter* — (*starting to sing*) "lead me to the altar —" ...

On the sofa, Clive laughs happily, enjoying this recital. Walter looks across at Clive, deeply embarrassed. Clive is laughing so much that he has to bury his face in a cushion

Walter (*whispering to Jemma*) You mustn't sing that!

Jemma Don't you like my singing?

Walter Yes, I ... I like it well enough. But you mustn't sing *that* song! Not in front of Clive! You'll make him jealous.

Jemma Will I?

Walter Yes! Sylvia told me all about you and ... (*He indicates Clive*)

Jemma (*wearily*) Oh — yes — I'd forgotten ...! (*She turns and trots back to Clive, arms outstretched*) Oh, Clive ...!

Clive emerges from the cushion and sees her approaching at speed

Clive Oh, no ...!

He leaps up and hops away. Jemma pursues him around the furniture. Walter watches the chase, laughing happily. Jemma's running is too much for

Clive's hopping and she catches him and clasps him to her bosom on the sofa. He struggles, manfully

No! You don't want me! You want Walter!
Jemma Oh — yes — right ...!

Jemma is finding it hard to keep up with her two personae, and staggers frantically from one to the other, while Walter and Clive watch her in total amazement

Jemma Oh, Walter — Oh, Clive — Oh, Walter — Oh, Clive — Oh, Walter — Oh, God ...! (*She sinks, exhausted, on to the sofa*)
Walter Well, I'm going into the kitchen ...

He goes quickly into the kitchen

Clive So am I! (*He hops hastily into the kitchen after Walter*)

Jemma is trying to get her breath back. Then she sees that the men have gone

Jemma Oh, no! They mustn't talk to each other! (*Wearily*) Here I go again ...!

She gets up and staggers out after the men. They disappear into the back of the kitchen

Eddie and Sylvia come out of Bedroom 2

Eddie Well, I'd never have guessed! Fancy your friend having a lover! But why doesn't she take him back to her *own* flat?
Sylvia Because her flat's in Ponders End, and her husband's in it.
Eddie And why is her lover dressed in shorts?
Sylvia Because he always arrives by boat.
Eddie What?!
Sylvia Up the river! (*She mimes rowing*)
Eddie Oh — I see! He comes here by boat so he can make a quick getaway if her husband turns up from Ponders End?
Sylvia Well ... yes, exactly!
Eddie (*considering*) But, Sylv ...

Sylvia Yes?

Eddie If you've lent your flat to Jemma tonight ... what are *you* doing here?

Sylvia Oh — er — Clive shouldn't have been here tonight! It was a mistake. He ... he arrived unexpectedly.

Eddie What about the other bloke?

Sylvia Walter?

Eddie Yes!

Sylvia Ah ... well ... *he* wasn't supposed to be here, either.

Eddie (*desperately*) But who *is* he?

Sylvia tries hard to think of a suitable explanation

Sylvia Er ... well, he's ... he's ... he's Jemma's husband!

Eddie stares at her, appalled

Eddie Her *husband*?

Sylvia Yes.

Eddie He's not in Ponders End, then?

Sylvia No. He's here.

Eddie Oh, my God ...! (*Visualizing the scene*) So — her husband turned up and found them together — Clive made a dash for his boat — twisted his ankle — and that's why he's limping!

Sylvia (*having reached the point of no return*) Well ... yes.

Eddie Oh, Sylv — what a little drama you've got going on here!

Sylvia Yes. I have, haven't I?

Eddie Lucky you was here. There might have been violence.

Sylvia There still might ...!

Eddie And they're both in there? *Together*?

Sylvia Well, they were supposed to be making sandwiches ...

Eddie I'd better keep them apart! (*He hastens towards the kitchen door*)

Sylvia (*calling after him*) You don't have to do that!

Eddie bustles into the kitchen, closing the door after him. Sylvia sits on the sofa in despair, sees Walter's whisky and downs it in one. Lights out in the sitting-room

Lights up in the kitchen. Jemma, Walter and Clive are coming in from

*the unseen part of the kitchen with plates of sandwiches which they put
down on the table to sort and count. They see Eddie*

Clive Now here's another one! Soon we'll *all* be in the kitchen!

Eddie (*incredulously*) Blimey, you really *are* making sandwiches!

Jemma Well, we're all very hungry. And there'll be a troop of Boy Scouts
arriving before long. So we've got to be prepared.

Eddie How can you make sandwiches at a time like this?

Walter I don't see that it's any of your business. Cucumbers have nothing
to do with carpentry.

Eddie You're taking it all very calmly.

Walter Well, I never could get very excited over a cucumber.

Eddie (*taking Jemma aside a little*) They ... they haven't been arguing,
then?

Jemma Oh, no. I think the vote was unanimous.

Eddie (*puzzled*) Vote?

Jemma Tomato or cucumber for the sandwiches.

Eddie It's all been ... peaceful so far, then?

Jemma Oh, yes.

Eddie I expect that's just the calm before the storm ...

Jemma What storm?

Eddie Must have been quite a shock for you when he turned up.

Jemma Sorry?

Eddie Don't you worry. *I'll* get him out of here.

*Eddie goes and grabs Walter by the arm and pulls him towards the door.
They all look surprised*

   Come on!

Walter What the hell are you doing?

Eddie You're not staying in here! (*He opens the door*) We can't have
fisticuffs — not in front of Jemma!

He pushes Walter through into the sitting-room and slams the door

   Lucky I came in when I did, eh?

Jemma Yes. Walter was buttering far too much bread.

Eddie Fancy him turning up like that, eh?

Jemma Who?

Eddie Your old man!

Jemma I beg your pardon?

Eddie And all the time you thought he was safely stowed away in Ponders End.

Jemma What do *you* know about Ponders End?

Eddie I know someone who isn't there! (*To Clive*) He didn't give you much time to get to the lifeboat, then?

Clive (*mystified*) What lifeboat?

Eddie Isn't that what you were doing when you twisted your ankle? Making a dash for it?

Jemma What are you talking about?

Eddie Your husband, of course!

Jemma Don't tell me *he's* here, as well!

Eddie Of course he's here! He's out there talking to Sylv.

Jemma What?!

She races across to bend down and look through the keyhole

Lights up in the sitting-room

Walter Why don't you get rid of the bloody carpenter, leave Jemma and Clive to get on with it and come away with me tonight?

Sylvia Where to?

Walter Paris. Bellagio. Tunbridge Wells.

Sylvia (*tempted*) Paris? Bellagio? (*Then, firmly*) No, Walter!

Walter All right — Tunbridge Wells it is! (*He tries to lead her away*)

Sylvia (*wavering*) It is tempting ... I do love you, Walter.

Walter And I love you. That's all that matters. (*He tries again, but she resists*)

Sylvia But I don't know how *much* I love you.

Walter At this rate we'll never find out! I'd be good for you, Sylvia.

Sylvia Oh, yes. I know you would. You're solid, reliable, dependable, successful ...

Walter Keep going till you get to attractive, adorable, romantic and sexy.

Sylvia (*giggling*) You don't look very sexy in that apron!

Walter hastily takes off the apron and casts it aside. Lights out in the sitting-room

In the kitchen ...

Jemma (*straightening up*) That's not my husband!
Eddie Of course it is!
Jemma I do know what my own husband looks like.
Eddie Well, Sylv said it was your husband.

Jemma stares at him, blankly, for a moment

Jemma What?
Eddie *Sylvia* said it was your husband.
Jemma Did she?
Eddie Yes!

Jemma realizes. She bends quickly to look through the keyhole again, then straightens up, decisively

Jemma It *is* my husband! I didn't recognize him without his hat on.
Clive (*to Eddie*) What the hell's her husband doing here?
Eddie He's come to see what you're up to!
Clive It's none of his business.
Eddie What?!
Jemma Of course it is, Clive!
Clive (*bewildered*) Why should your husband care about what *I'm* up to?

Jemma goes to him and takes his arm, heavily affectionate

Jemma Oh, Clive ... You don't have to pretend just because the carpenter's here. I don't mind if he finds out ...

Clive looks glassy

Eddie And I *have* found out! Sylv told me all about it.
Clive (*to Jemma*) I still don't see what it's got to do with your husband ...
Eddie Blimey, what do you expect from him? A round of applause? (*To Jemma*) We'd better get him out of here.
Jemma Which one?
Eddie *This* one, of course!
Jemma Good idea ...!
Eddie You go and make sure your husband stays in there while Clive makes his getaway.
Clive What getaway?

Jemma Oh, Clive, don't be so difficult! There's bound to be a drain pipe outside the window. You can climb down that.

Clive looks aghast

Clive How am I going to climb down a drain pipe with this? (*He waves his bad foot in the air*)

Jemma Oh — yes — that might be a bit tricky. (*To Eddie*) We'll have to find another way to get him out of here.

Clive I don't want to get out of here! I just want everyone *else* to get out of here!

Eddie (*to Jemma*) I know! You persuade your husband to go into the bedroom with you.

Jemma How shall I do that?

Eddie You must have done it before! Even in Ponders End.

Jemma Well, I'll do my best ...

Eddie (*to Clive*) Once her husband's out of the way you can hop out of the front door and get a taxi back to the boathouse.

Clive I'm not going to the boathouse!

Jemma Well, you can't stay here all night.

Eddie No. If her husband sets eyes on you again he may not be able to control himself.

Clive (*glaring at Eddie*) Look — I don't know what all this has got to do with *you*, anyway! You're only here to build a cupboard!

Jemma Now, now, boys — you mustn't start fighting! (*To Eddie*) *You*'d better come with me!

She grabs Eddie's arm and drags him out into the sitting-room. Clive watches them go, bemused. Lights out in the kitchen

Lights up in the sitting-room. Walter and Sylvia look up as Jemma and Eddie come out of the kitchen. Jemma releases Eddie and goes, briskly, across to Walter

Jemma Come along, Walter! (*She grabs Walter's hand and starts to lead him towards the bedrooms*)

Walter Where are we going?

Jemma Into the bedroom!

Walter I'm not going into a bedroom with you! You're bad enough in front of the freezer.

Jemma Oh, come on, Walter!

Eddie Yes — we know it's been a nasty shock for you, finding out about her and Clive, but can't you forgive and forget?

Walter (*astonished*) I beg your pardon?

Sylvia Yes, Walter — kiss and make up!

Walter What are you talking about?

Jemma There's something I want to show you in the bedroom.

Walter Well, I don't want to see it!

Eddie (*crossing to Walter*) Don't be daft, Walter! You must have seen it before. Come on! It'll only take a minute. (*He urges Walter towards Bedroom 2*)

Walter No! (*He struggles with Eddie*)

Jemma (*whispering to Sylvia*) So I'm Walter's *wife* now, then am I?

Sylvia (*whispering also*) Well, I had to tell Eddie *some*thing ...

Jemma pulls Sylvia to her feet and starts to lead her towards the kitchen

Walter (*glaring at Eddie*) Sylvia and I were in the middle of a private conversation.

Eddie Well, it'll have to wait, won't it? You mustn't keep your lady waiting. (*He tries to urge him on*)

Jemma (*quietly, as they go*) I'm going to get Walter out of the way. You go and tell Clive that it's all clear for him to hop off home.

Walter Let go of me! I'm not going into a bedroom with that woman!

Eddie All right, then you'll have to go with me!

Walter No fear!

They struggle

Sylvia (*quietly, to Jemma*) Is Clive *going* to hop off home, then?

Jemma Of course he is! (*She opens the kitchen door*)

Sylvia Oh, good!

Jemma pushes Sylvia into the kitchen and returns to the others

Walter I'm not going in there with him!

Eddie I only want to show you my cupboard.

Jemma Yes — you can give him your advice.

Walter What advice?

Jemma About how to do it!

Walter I thought he was a carpenter. He's supposed to *know* how to do it. I'm a solicitor, and I don't expect him to advise me about conveyancing!

Jemma He only wants your opinion.

Eddie I might be making it too big.

Walter At the moment you're not making it at all! (*To Jemma*) I'm not going into a bedroom with an incompetent carpenter.

Jemma All right, then, Eddie — you go ahead.

Eddie Sorry?

Jemma Then Walter and I can be left on our own to kiss and make up ... (*She advances on him, hungrily*)

Walter No fear! I'd sooner go with *him*!

Walter races out into Bedroom 2. Eddie grins at Jemma, gives the "thumbs-up" sign, and goes out after Walter, closing the door behind him. Jemma hastens towards the kitchen

Lights up in the kitchen. Sylvia is trying to encourage Clive to leave

Sylvia Come on, Clive! It's all clear!

Clive All clear for what?

Sylvia For you to hop off home, of course!

Clive I'm not going to hop off home!

Sylvia I thought you wanted to?

Jemma arrives from the sitting-room

Jemma Hurry up, Clive! There isn't much time!

Sylvia He doesn't want to go.

Jemma Of course he wants to go! (*To Clive*) My husband's here!

Clive *I* don't care. (*He chuckles*) I hope you haven't left him out there with Walter!

Jemma Oh, no. Walter's in the spare room with the carpenter.

Sylvia looks alarmed

Sylvia You mean they're together?

Jemma Yes. (*Then she realizes and looks at Sylvia*)

Jemma ⎫
Sylvia ⎬ (*together*) They may be talking to each other!
Jemma (*wearily*) Oh, here I go again ...!

Jemma races out into the sitting-room, hesitates for a moment to catch her breath, and then staggers out into Bedroom 2, slamming the door behind her

Sylvia and Clive are alone in the kitchen

Clive Why don't you get rid of the bloody carpenter, leave Jemma and Walter to sort it all out and come away with me tonight?
Sylvia Where to?
Clive I don't care where it is as long as you run away with me.
Sylvia You couldn't run very far on that ankle.
Clive Well ... when my ankle's better.
Sylvia (*wavering*) It is tempting ... I do love you, Clive.
Clive And I love you. That's all that matters.

He starts to lead her away, forgetting his bad ankle, and cries out in agony

Clive Ooooh! (*He sits down again in pain*) I know I'd be good for you, Sylvia — once I'm back on my feet again.
Sylvia Yes. You probably would. But I've got to be certain, haven't I? And I ... I just can't make up my mind ...

They gaze at each other, bleakly

In the sitting-room ...

The door to Bedroom 2 opens and Jemma comes out, pulling Walter behind her

Walter I wish you'd make up your mind! A minute ago you wanted me to go *into* the spare room. (*He goes towards the kitchen*) Is Sylvia out in the kitchen?
Jemma Yes, but ——
Walter Right! (*He continues on his way*)

Jemma races around and intercepts him, her arms outstretched

Jemma No! You can't go in there!
Walter (*wearily*) Oh, don't start all that again ...

Jemma pushes him back to the sofa and plonks him down, abruptly

Jemma *You* stay in here! *I'*ll go in there! I'll say you're in here! (*She darts out into the kitchen, closing the door behind her*)

Walter picks up his whisky glass in despair, sees that it is now empty, and looks puzzled

In the kitchen ...

Jemma bursts in

Jemma It's all right! He's in the sitting-room!
Sylvia (*relieved*) Oh, good ...
Clive *Who*'s in the sitting-room?
Jemma (*breathlessly*) Walter. And Eddie's in the spare room. And you're in here. Isn't that a splendid arrangement? One man in each room.
Clive What about your husband?
Jemma What husband?
Sylvia Surely you haven't forgotten your *husband*!
Jemma (*remembering*) Oh — my husband! — him! — yes! He's in the sitting-room, as well.
Clive (*fearfully*) Talking to Walter?
Jemma Er ... yes. In a way.

She grins at Sylvia. They freeze

In the sitting-room ...

Eddie comes in from Bedroom 2. Walter looks far from pleased to see him

Eddie Here — I want to give you a bit of advice.
Walter I don't want your advice!
Eddie If I were you, I'd forgive and forget. I'm sure you're not really a violent man.

Walter (*glaring at him*) Don't be *too* sure about that!

Eddie So why not buy her a bunch of flowers and give her a great big kiss?

Walter (*puzzled*) Who?

Eddie Jemma, of course!

Walter I'll do no such thing.

Eddie She'd appreciate it.

Walter Yes. I'm sure she would. But I'm not in the habit of going around kissing strange ladies and thrusting flowers at them.

Eddie (*sadly*) Oh, dear. Worse than I thought. Already you've become strangers to each other.

Walter (*bemused*) What?

In the kitchen ...

Clive (*to Jemma*) Aren't you going to go in there and separate them?

Jemma Who?

Clive Walter and your husband!

Jemma I don't think I *could* ...! (*She grins at Sylvia*)

Clive But if he knows what's been going on between you and Walter, they might be coming to blows.

Jemma I doubt it ...!

Clive Well, I'm sure I heard raised voices.

Sylvia (*alarmed*) Did you? (*She looks at Jemma*)

Jemma Oh, my God ...!

Jemma hastens to the door and bends down to look through the keyhole

In the sitting-room ...

Walter You're not here to give advice! You're here to build a bloody cupboard!

Eddie (*with a grin*) Well ... not just that.

Walter What?

Eddie I'm here because I want to marry her!

Walter Who?

Eddie Who do you think? (*He jerks his head towards the kitchen*)

Walter Not ...?

Eddie Yes!

Walter starts to laugh

Walter Oh, no! Not you, as well! She *is* a dark horse! And do you always meet in Sylvia's flat?
Eddie Yes.
Walter How often?
Eddie Once a fortnight.
Walter (*smiling, broadly*) My dear fellow — join the club! (*He shakes Eddie's hand*)

Eddie is surprised

In the kitchen ...

Jemma (*straightening up*) They're shaking hands!
Clive Walter and your husband?
Jemma No! Walter and the carpenter.
Sylvia You mean Walter and Eddie are both in the sitting-room?
Jemma (*calmly*) Yes. They're talking to each ... (*She stops and looks at Sylvia in alarm*)
Jemma ⎱ (*together*) They're talking to each other!
Sylvia ⎰

Jemma and Sylvia race out into the sitting-room. Clive watches them go, bewildered. Lights out in the kitchen

In the sitting-room ...

Walter and Eddie are shaking hands as Jemma and Sylvia come bursting in

Jemma Eddie! I left you in the spare room!
Eddie I was trying to get him to buy you some flowers.
Jemma (*touched*) Oh, what a lovely thought ...
Eddie But he won't.
Jemma Oh, Walter! Why not?
Walter (*laughing*) I should think you've got enough men buying you flowers already!
Jemma Have I? (*She exchanges a puzzled look with Sylvia*)
Walter Do you think that Clive suspects?
Sylvia (*blankly*) Suspects what?
Walter That Eddie isn't here just to build a cupboard! (*He laughs*)

Sylvia (*nervously*) Walter, what *are* you talking about? Of course he's here to build a cupboard.
Walter No, he's not! He's here because he wants to marry Jemma!

They all react. Quite a pause. Then Sylvia turns to Jemma with a big smile

Sylvia Jemma — darling! What a lovely surprise! You never told me that.
Jemma Didn't I? It must have slipped my mind ...
Eddie Now just hang on a minute!
Walter (*to Eddie*) Where did you meet her, then? In Sylvia's shop?
Eddie Meet her? I've never even *seen* her before!
Walter (*enjoying it enormously*) And yet you still want to marry her?
Jemma It was love at first sight, wasn't it, Eddie?

Clive hops in from the kitchen. Eddie looks at him in surprise

Eddie You should have gone by now!
Clive I'm not going anywhere while *you're* still in this flat!

Which remark Walter, understandably, misunderstands

Walter So you *do* know about Eddie?
Jemma No! No, he doesn't!
Clive (*blankly*) Sorry?
Walter Well, I suppose you'd be bound to have found out sooner or later.
Clive Found out what?
Walter (*heavily*) That the carpenter wants to marry Jemma as well.
Clive (*amused*) *What?*
Eddie Now just a minute!

Jemma hastily grabs Eddie in a fond embrace

Jemma Oh, Eddie, you've swept me off my feet! Why don't you carry me away into the night?
Eddie (*laughing*) I think Clive's the one who ought to do that!
Clive *Me?* (*He laughs*)
Eddie Look, there's something I'd like to explain to you all ——
Jemma No, Eddie! It's far too late for carpentry lessons.
Clive (*to Sylvia*) Does her husband know that she's got two men on the go?

Sylvia Two? It was three at the last count ...!
Clive And is that why he's gone?
Sylvia Who?
Clive Jemma's husband!
Sylvia Ah — yes! Yes — he went ages ago!
Eddie No, he didn't!
Jemma Yes, he did! He said he had to get back to Ponders End!
Eddie Don't be daft! He's still here!
Clive (*looking about*) Where?
Eddie Here! (*indicating Walter*) *This* is Jemma's husband!

A dreadful pause. Reactions

Jemma Shall we go and see to the sandwiches, Sylvia?
Walter Don't be ridiculous!
Jemma Oh, I thought it was quite a good idea ...
Eddie You mean ... you're *not* her husband?
Walter Of course I'm not!

Jemma and Sylvia start to tiptoe away

Clive ⎱
　　　　(*together*) Just a minute!
Eddie ⎰

The girls stop and turn, sheepishly

Eddie You said ...
Sylvia I was confused.
Clive And *you* said ...
Jemma I made a mistake.
Clive How could you make a mistake about your own husband?
Jemma Well, you try identifying someone through a keyhole!

Walter has had a thought

Walter But Eddie ...
Eddie Yes?
Walter If you thought I was Jemma's husband, why on earth did you tell
　　me that you wanted to marry her?
Eddie Not Jemma! Sylvia!

They all react

Walter *This* Sylvia?
Eddie Yes.
Walter You want to marry ... Sylvia?
Eddie Yes!

Jemma tries to save the situation and turns to Sylvia

Jemma You see? This is what happens if you let carpenters work in the evening. They start falling in love with you.
Clive (*to Sylvia, amused*) Did you *know* that the carpenter wanted to marry you?
Sylvia Well ... he did say something about it.
Walter (*also amused*) And what did you tell him?
Eddie She said she was thinking it over.
Walter } (*together, no longer amused*) What?!
Clive
Sylvia Well, I didn't want to discourage him.
Jemma No. Otherwise he'd never finish that cupboard!
Eddie There's something I don't understand ...
Jemma I thought there might be!
Eddie (*to Walter*) If you're *not* Jemma's husband, what the hell are you doing in Sylvia's flat?
Walter I don't see that it's any of your business, but if you must know I——
Sylvia He came to watch the match!
Eddie What match?
Sylvia The football match! On the television!
Jemma They lost. Three-nil.
Eddie Hasn't he got a television of his own?
Sylvia It's out of order!
Eddie Why didn't he ring a repair man?
Jemma His telephone's out of order as well!
Clive His television *and* his telephone?
Jemma Yes. It *was* an unlucky day for him, wasn't it?
Walter Look, there's something I——
Eddie Are you trying to tell me that Walter only came here to watch the television?

Sylvia Yes!

Jemma She heard the front door bell go, you see? So she answered it. Well, you would, wouldn't you? If you heard the front doorbell go. You wouldn't just ignore it. Might be important. So she did. And when she opened the door — there was this total stranger! Just standing there. Like a postman. So they got into conversation. You know how it is. And he said to her — and you're going to find this very difficult to believe at first — he said to her, " I'm sorry to bother you at this time of night. I hope I haven't interrupted your dinner. But my television's out of order, and I can't get a repair man because my telephone's out of order. And I don't want to miss the football match so can I come in and watch it with you?" And she said yes. Well, what would *you* say to a desperate man on your doorstep dying for football?

They are all astonished by this speedy exposition

Walter I beg your pardon?

Jemma I'm not saying all that again ...!

Eddie You don't expect me to believe all that, do you? (*To Walter*) Why did you *really* come here?

Clive (*impatiently*) Oh, for heaven's sake! Because he's having an affair with Jemma, of course.

Jemma and Sylvia look at each other in despair. Walter is amused at the thought

Walter Whatever gave you that idea?

Clive You mean it isn't true?

Walter You know very well it isn't true. You're the one who's having an affair with Jemma!

Clive Who ever told you that?

Walter Sylvia, of course!

Sylvia Can I get anyone a little hot soup?

Walter (*to Clive*) You mean you're *not* having an affair with Jemma?

Clive Of course I'm not!

Jemma Oh, dear. A moment ago I had *three* lovers. Now I've got none ...

Walter But if you didn't come here to see Jemma, who the hell *did* you come to see?

Clive Sylvia, of course!

Walter and Eddie react

Walter You rowed a mile and a half up the river to see *Sylvia*?
Clive Yes.
Walter Why?
Clive Because I want to marry her!
Walter (*to Sylvia*) Did *you* know that?
Sylvia Well ... he did say something about it.
Walter He's got a damn nerve! I hope you told him where to get off.
Clive She said she was thinking it over.
Walter ⎫
Eddie ⎭ (*together*) What?!
Walter (*to Clive*) You mean ... that when you come here once a fortnight
   ... you come to see ... *Sylvia*?
Clive Yes! On a Friday ...
Eddie What?!
Walter So do I! On a Wednesday ...
Clive What?!
Eddie So do I! On a Monday ...
Walter ⎫
Clive ⎭ (*together*) What?!
Jemma I could always pop out for a Chinese takeaway.

The men turn to face Sylvia. She cowers

Walter All *three* of us?
Sylvia Yes ...
Clive All at the same time?
Sylvia (*defensively*) On different nights!
Walter No wonder you couldn't see us more than once a fortnight ...
Clive And that's why Jemma suddenly found she'd got two lovers?
Jemma Yes. I thought I'd won the football pools.
Sylvia I just wasn't expecting you all on the same day!

A pause. The men contemplate. Then Sylvia suddenly leaps up in front of them and holds her hands above her head, dramatically

   You mustn't *fight* over me!

The men are silent and still, not even considering violence

Jemma I don't think they're going to.

Sylvia (*rather put out*) Aren't they? (*To the men*) Aren't you?

Eddie How could you carry on with three blokes at the same time?

Sylvia Because I love you *all*! But I couldn't make up my mind which of you I wanted to marry ...

Jemma And that's why she's been having you all on approval.

Walter turns, solemnly, to the other men

Walter I think we'd better go into the kitchen.

Clive }
Eddie }   (*together*) Good idea!

They go to the kitchen door. Walter looks back at Sylvia

Walter This won't take very long.

The men go into the kitchen, closing the door behind them. Lights up faintly in the kitchen

Sylvia What are they going to do?

Jemma (*with a shrug*) Russian roulette?

Sylvia (*hopefully*) Perhaps they *are* going to fight over me?

Jemma and Sylvia hasten to the kitchen door. Jemma bends down to peer through the keyhole. Sylvia hovers behind her

In the kitchen we can see the vague shapes of the men huddled together, talking soundlessly

Are they hitting each other?

Jemma No. I don't think so.

Sylvia (*aggrieved*) Why not? You said if they found out they'd murder each other.

Jemma Good heavens!

Sylvia What are they doing?

Jemma I think they're eating cucumber sandwiches. (*A moment, then she laughs*) Oh, no ...!

Sylvia What's happening?

Jemma Walter seems to be saying "Eeny-meeny-miney-mo ..."

Sylvia What a cheek! *I'm* the one who's supposed to make the choice.
Jemma Ah! They're coming back.

Sylvia and Jemma rush away from the kitchen door and take up more relaxed positions. The men return as the Lights go out in the kitchen. They take up positions in a row facing Sylvia, self-conciously

Walter Er ... we've discussed the matter carefully, the ... the three of us ... and we've come to a decision.
Jemma You didn't take very long about it.
Eddie That's because we're unanimous.
Sylvia (*coldly*) And what ... decision ... have the three of you come to?
Clive We've decided ... to carry on as we are.

A beat

Sylvia I *beg* your pardon?
Eddie We've all agreed ... to go on sharing you.
Sylvia (*astonished*) *Sharing* me?
Walter On one condition. It'll have to be equal time for all.
Jemma Like a party political broadcast?
Sylvia (*seething*) You're all prepared to go on ... sharing me?
Clive ⎫
Eddie ⎬ (*together*) Yes.
Walter ⎭
Sylvia How *dare* you!
Eddie We thought you'd be pleased.
Sylvia I've never heard anything so immoral in all my life!
Jemma Neither have I! (*Then, with a smile*) But it does sound rather nice...
Walter But *you*'ve been sharing *us*.
Sylvia That's different! I was deciding.
Clive Well, *we*'ve decided.
Eddie Yes. A third each.
Sylvia A third each?!
Jemma (*to Sylvia*) That might work out rather well. Nothing like a bit of competition. They'll all be trying hard to outdo each other.
Clive Yes! Think of all the chocolates you'll get!
Walter And the flowers!
Eddie And the cupboards!
Sylvia Well, I think you're all dreadful!

The front doorbell rings

Jemma Now I suppose the Boy Scouts have turned up!

Jemma hastens out to the front door

The three men face Sylvia, glumly

Eddie You see, Sylv — none of us wants to lose you ...

Walter
Clive } (*together*) No ...

Clive Because we all love you ...

Walter
Eddie } (*together*) Yes ...

Walter So if we can't have you *all* of the time, we'd rather have you part of the time than not have you at all ...

Eddie
Clive } (*together*) Yes ...

Sylvia gazes at them, obviously moved

An enormous bunch of flowers comes in from the hall, completely hiding Jemma, who is carrying it. The others watch in surprise as it approaches. It stops, and Jemma's face peers around the side of the flowers

Jemma A gentleman has brought you a few flowers.
Sylvia (*at a loss*) W ... what gentleman?

Jemma gives her an old-fashioned look

Jemma You'll *never* guess ...
Sylvia (*guessing*) Robin!
Jemma How ever did you guess?
Sylvia Well ... what did he say?
Jemma He said he's sorry, how about dinner, and he'll be waiting outside with his engine running.

Sylvia tries her best to appear undecided

Sylvia tries her best to appear undecided

Sylvia Oh, Jemma — what *am* I going to do?
Jemma You know very well what you're going to do. And I should do it quickly before he changes his mind again!

Sylvia runs to the three men, who are standing in a row, disconsolately, and kisses each of them in turn

Sylvia Oh, Walter ... (*kiss*) Oh, Eddie ... (*kiss*) Oh, Clive ...(*kiss*) I am sorry. Really I am. But you see, Robin's the one man I always *knew* I wanted to marry. (*She takes the flowers from Jemma and runs towards the hall, happily*)
Walter Sylvia ...

Sylvia stops and looks at them

Sylvia Yes?

The men smile at her, warmly

Walter Good luck, then ...
Clive Yes — good luck ...
Eddie Good luck, Sylv ...
Sylvia (*near to tears*) Oh, Jemma — aren't men *wonderful*?

She exits quickly, carrying the enormous bunch of flowers

The men are left standing in uncertain, sombre silence

Jemma Would anyone like a cucumber sandwich?

No takers. The men stir, haphazardly. Music fades in softly

Eddie Well, I ...I'll just fetch my gear ...

He wanders in a dream into Bedroom 2

Walter Come on, then, Clive. I'll give you a lift to the boathouse. (*He collects his briefcase and — with a sad smile — his raincoat*)

Jemma (*starting to cry*) Oh, I can't bear it ...!

Eddie returns with his toolbag and a few odd pieces of wood

Eddie Oh ... er ... tell Sylv I'll call her. You know — about the cupboard.
Jemma Yes ... right ...
Walter   Well ... goodbye, Jemma.

Clive and Eddie mutter their goodbyes

Clive }
Eddie }   (*together*) 'Bye, Jemma ...
Jemma Goodbye ... (*She snuffles, sadly, into her handkerchief*)

The three men start to drift, dejectedly, towards the hall. Jemma has a sudden thought, and cheers up, abruptly

Wait a minute!

The men stop, their backs to her

I've just had a *marvellous* idea! (*She smiles, broadly*) Why don't you all share *me*?

They turn, in unison, and look at her in surprise

Black-out

CURTAIN

GROUND PLAN

to rest of kitchen

to front door and dining-room

chair

kitchen table

chair

fridge

kitchen units

cut-away wall

door

drinks cupboard

T.V.

armchair

interior backing

arch

coffee table

sofa

table

chair

garden table

steps up

chair

rostrum

sky backing

chest

bedroom 1

bedroom 2

steps down

chair

backing

backing

FURNITURE AND PROPERTY LIST

ACT I

On stage: *Sitting-room*:
Sofa. *On it*: cushions
Sofa table. *On it*: 2 wine glasses, bottle of wine (open), ice bucket,
    bowl of fruit (including 1 banana)
Small coffee table
Television table. *On it*: TV set
Small armchair
Upright chair
Chest. *In it*: travelling rug
Drinks cupboard. *On it*: dish of nuts
In it: whisky, gin, tonics, opener, glasses
Sylvia's handbag. *In it*: £10 note
Curtains (practical)
Carpet

Balcony:
Small garden table
2 garden chairs

Kitchen:
Kitchen units. *On them or in them*: coffee mug, jar of coffee, spoon,
    tin of biscuits, plate
Fridge. *In it:* bottle of milk, 2 cans of lager
Small table
2 kitchen chairs
Key in door
Metal tray
Tiled floor

Off stage: Weekend bag (**Jemma**)
Duty free bag (full) (**Jemma**)
Handbag (**Jemma**)
Matching mug of coffee (**Sylvia**)
Raincoat (**Clive**)

Briefcase (**Walter**)
Bunch of flowers (**Walter**)
Bread and cheese (**Walter**)
Bits of wood (**Eddie**)
Bag of tools (**Eddie**)

Personal: **Clive**: box of chocolates, wrist-watch
Sylvia: wrist-watch
Walter: wrist-watch

ACT II

On stage: *Sitting-room*:
Dish of nuts
Flower in vase

Kitchen:
Dish of nuts
Dustpan and brush

Off stage: Mug of coffee (**Jemma**)
Clothes (**Jemma**)
Colourful kitchen apron (**Walter**)
3 plates of sandwiches (**Jemma, Walter, and Clive**)
Extra large bunch of flowers (**Jemma**)
Bits of wood (**Eddie**)
Bag of tools (**Eddie**)

LIGHTING PLOT

Property fittings required: nil
Interior. A composite set of a sitting-room and part of a kitchen. The same scene throughout.

ACT I A summer evening

To open: Black-out

Cue 1	**As** CURTAIN **rises** *Lights up in all areas*	(Page 1)
Cue 2	**Clive sits, disconsolately** *Lights out in kitchen*	(Page 5)
Cue 3	**Sylvia goes into the kitchen** *Lights up in kitchen*	(Page 7)
Cue 4	**Clive sits down in despair** *Lights out in kitchen*	(Page 9)
Cue 5	**As Sylvia goes into the kitchen** *Lights up in kitchen*	(Page 10)
Cue 6	**Sylvia draws the curtains** *Fade sitting-room area slightly*	(Page 11)
Cue 7	**Sylvia opens the curtains** *Fade sitting-room area up again*	(Page 12)
Cue 8	**Sylvia goes into the sitting-room** *Lights out in kitchen*	(Page 13)
Cue 9	**Walter switches the TV on** *Fade up TV light effect*	(Page 17)
Cue 10	**Sylvia switches the TV off** *Cut TV light effect*	(Page 18)

EFFECTS PLOT

ACT I

ACT II

Lightning Source UK Ltd.
Milton Keynes UK
UKOW06f2347180117
292339UK00014B/201/P

9 780573 017490